MAROONED *in the* ARCTIC

Other Books in the Women of Action Series

Code Name Pauline by Pearl Witherington Cornioley,
edited by Kathryn J. Atwood

Double Victory by Cheryl Mullenbach

The Many Faces of Josephine Baker by Peggy Caravantes

Reporting Under Fire by Kerrie L. Hollihan

She Takes a Stand by Michael Elsohn Ross

Women Aviators by Karen Bush Gibson

Women Heroes of the American Revolution by Susan Casey

Women Heroes of World War I by Kathryn J. Atwood

Women Heroes of World War II by Kathryn J. Atwood

Women in Space by Karen Bush Gibson

Women of Colonial American by Brandon Marie Miller

Women of Steel and Stone by Anna M. Lewis

Women of the Frontier by Brandon Marie Miller

A World of Her Own by Michael Elsohn Ross

MAROONED
in the ARCTIC

THE TRUE STORY OF ADA BLACKJACK,
THE "FEMALE ROBINSON CRUSOE"

PEGGY CARAVANTES

CHICAGO
REVIEW
PRESS

Published by Chicago Review Press Incorporated
814 North Franklin Street
Chicago, Illinois 60610
ISBN 978-1-61373-098-0

Library of Congress Cataloging-in-Publication Data

Names: Caravantes, Peggy, 1935- author.
Title: Marooned in the Arctic : the true story of Ada Blackjack, the "female
    Robinson Crusoe" / Peggy Caravantes.
Description: Chicago, Illinois : Chicago Review Press, 2016. | Series:
    Women of action | Includes bibliographical references and index.
Identifiers: LCCN 2015029636 | ISBN 9781613730980 (hardback)
Subjects: LCSH: Blackjack, Ada, 1898-1983—Juvenile literature. | Inuit
    women—Biography—Juvenile literature. | Women explorers—Arctic
    regions—Biography—Juvenile literature. | Arctic regions—Discovery
    and exploration—Juvenile literature. | Wrangel Island (Russia)—Dis-
    covery and exploration—Juvenile literature. | BISAC: JUVENILE
    NONFICTION / Biography & Autobiography / Women. | JUVENILE
    NONFICTION / Biography & Autobiography / Historical. | JUVENILE
    NONFICTION / Adventure & Adventurers. | JUVENILE NONFIC-
    TION / Biography & Autobiography / Cultural Heritage.
Classification: LCC E99.E7 B65629 2016 | DDC 910.92—dc23 LC record
    available at http://lccn.loc.gov/2015029636

Interior design: Sarah Olson

Printed in the United States of America
5 4 3 2 1

Dedicated to the memory of my parents
John and Dorothy Garner Huddleston

CONTENTS

Author's Note ix
Map xi

1 IN THE BEGINNING. 1
Meet Vilhjalmur Stefansson. 19

2 SETTLING ON THE ISLAND 27
Meet Milton Galle. 45

3 CHANGING WINDS. 49
Meet Lorne Knight 66

4 FADING HOPES. 71
Meet Allan Crawford. 87

5 TREACHEROUS TREKS 91
Meet Frederick Maurer 101

6 OH FOR A BEAR! 105

7 DOWNWARD SPIRAL 115

8 RESCUE! 131

9 CONFLICT AND CONFUSION 149

AFTERWORD. 173

Acknowledgments. 175
Notes 177
Sources 187
Index 189

AUTHOR'S NOTE

MY PURPOSE IN WRITING this book is to share the story of Ada Blackjack Johnson, an incredibly courageous woman who became the only survivor of an Arctic expedition in the early 1920s. However, her story cannot be told without including the men who interacted with her. These were the expedition's sponsor, Vilhjalmur Stefansson, and the four men with whom she shared the experience—Allan Crawford, Lorne Knight, Frederick Maurer, and Milton Galle. Between each of the first six chapters is a short biography of one of the men. Most of Ada's story appears in the latter chapters because there is very little information available about her earlier life.

I have chosen to use the term *Eskimo*, rather than today's preferred *Inuit*, in referring to Ada because that was the terminology used at the time of her story. The men are mostly referred to by their last names and Ada by her first name; this was done to avoid confusion, as that is how they are discussed in the sources quoted.

Most of the story is based on the diaries of Lorne Knight and Ada Blackjack as well as on fragmentary notes written by Milton Galle. As the reader will learn at the end of the book, these manuscripts underwent some abuse before they were retrieved and eventually made part of the Stefansson Collection at Dartmouth College. Copies are all that are available today. In some cases there may be slight differences in the wording of various copies.

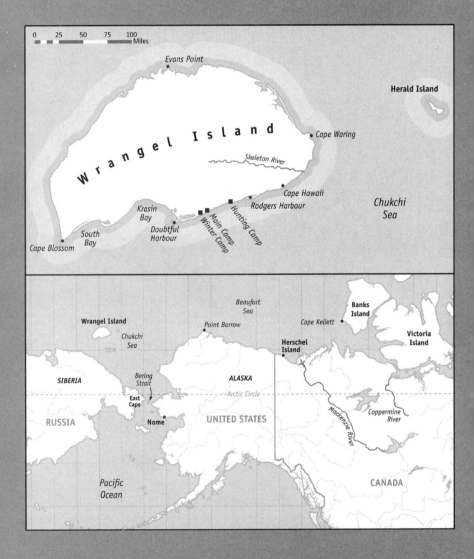

I

IN THE BEGINNING

ADA DELUTUK WAS BORN on May 10, 1898, in the remote settlement of Spruce Creek, eight miles from the small village of Solomon, Alaska. As a child she listened to stories passed down by her ancestors. Some of the tales taught her about stars in the sky. Others told about Nanook, the polar bear—the animal most feared by Eskimos. From an early age Ada developed a dread of being eaten by a polar bear and forever trapped in its stomach.

Imaginary fears turned into real troubles when Ada was eight years old. Her father died of food poisoning, and her mother sent her and her sister Rita to a Methodist mission school in Nome. (Ada had another sister, Fina, but it's not known when she was born or where she lived during this time.)

Leaving home at such an early age, Ada never learned the traditional skills of her people—skills she would desperately need in the future—such as hunting, trapping, fishing, firing a gun, living off the land, and building a shelter. Instead she was introduced to the skills that white society valued. She learned to read and write at an elementary level, to speak English (rather than her native Inuit language), to read the Bible, and to pray. She also received training in cleaning, cooking, sewing, and basic hygiene. The one Eskimo trait she did develop was the ability to sew animal furs into clothing.

Like most Eskimo girls, Ada married young, at the age of 16. The couple moved to the Seward Peninsula. After several gold rushes had emptied the mines there, the community had turned into a supplier of reindeer meat. The processing of huge herds required a great deal of manpower. Perhaps Ada's husband, Jack Blackjack, went to the Seward Peninsula to find such work. He had previously worked as a hunter and a dogsled driver.

The marriage did not go well. Not long after the wedding, Ada realized her husband had a cruel streak. She endured Jack beating her and starving her for six years because she wanted to protect their three children. After two of them died (the causes are unknown) Jack deserted her, leaving her and one son alone. Ada struggled with the devastating loss of her children and with caring for the surviving boy, Bennett, who had tuberculosis.

When Bennett was five years old, Ada divorced her husband before he could return and mistreat her again. She and her son moved to Nome, Alaska, where her mother then lived. Ada and Bennett made the entire 40-mile trip on foot. When the child was too tired to walk, his mother carried him. After reaching their destination, Ada eked out a living by cleaning houses and sewing clothes for miners.

But Bennett needed medical care she could not afford, so she placed him in the Jesse Lee Home for Children, a Methodist orphanage that accepted both parentless children and those whose parents could not care for them, often because of their own illness, such as tuberculosis, the most prevalent and most dreaded disease in Alaska at that time. Victims had to be placed in sanatoriums to lessen the spread of the disease, thus forcing their children into orphanages. Ada's driving focus became finding a better-paying job so she and Bennett could be together again.

One evening when Ada was on her way home from cleaning a house, E. R. Jordan, the police chief, stopped her as she walked by the station. He had known Ada most of her life and was familiar with the circumstances of her marriage and with Bennett's medical condition. He knew she needed money for her son's care, so he mentioned to her that a group of men were headed to Wrangel Island, a remote and uninhabited Arctic island almost 600 miles north of Nome, surrounded by the Chuchki Sea. The men were recruiting Eskimos to go with them to sew fur clothing while they were on the island. Ada was a superior seamstress, and her ability to speak English would be another plus. Jordan shared with her what he had heard about the trip north but at that time had no knowledge of the real purpose of the expedition.

Jordan told her that Vilhjalmur Stefansson, a noted Canadian and Arctic explorer, was organizing and arranging financing for the expedition, although he did not plan to participate. He would stay behind to continue fund-raising through his lecture tours and to seek private backing for another exploration to search for a continent north of Wrangel Island.

Stefansson personally selected four young men to represent him on the current exploration. He used his strong personality, reputation, and powers of persuasion to convince them to carry out the colonizing expedition while he remained at home. The chosen members included Errol Lorne Knight, a big, 28-year-old, outspoken, happy-go-lucky American from McMinnville, Oregon; he had been on a prior northern expedition with Stefansson. Frederick W. Maurer, another 28-year-old, from New Philadelphia, Ohio, had been a member of Stefansson's five-year Canadian expedition. Joining Maurer and Knight was their fellow countryman, 19-year-old Milton Galle, from New Braunfels, Texas, who was Stefansson's secretary when they traveled on the Chautauqua lecture circuit.

The fourth member was 20-year-old Canadian Allan R. Crawford, a student at the University of Toronto. An 1867 law classified all Canadians as British subjects, so Stefansson named Crawford as leader of the team. His British citizenship would be necessary to claim the island for Great Britain. Since Crawford had not been to the Arctic, his position was only nominal; Knight headed the team because of his previous experience. Stefansson told the men that he could afford to pay only minimal salaries—and nothing at all to young Galle, whom he had not planned to add to the expedition. For compensation, Galle could have a percentage of any furs that he brought back with him at the expedition's end. Despite that, all of them could hardly wait to start their trip and felt quite proud that Stefansson trusted them to carry out his mission.

The *Victoria* embarked from Seattle with the four young men aboard on August 18, 1921. Knight's parents were at the docks to see them off. The men promised they would write when they arrived at Nome, a voyage of four or five days. Those communications would be their last with their families until a relief ship was scheduled to go to Wrangel in 1922.

Stefansson swore the young men to secrecy about their true purpose in going to Wrangel Island. An excerpt from Galle's letter to Stefansson at that time illustrated the high spirits of the men as they deliberately misled passengers on the *Victoria* about their reason for going to the Arctic:

> From the time we left Seattle all those aboard asked as to our whereabouts this winter, Knight would answer one place Crawford another and Maurer still another and I said passed [sic] Point Barrow. I had most fun when in a bunch, Knight would be asked about some place around Hershall [sic] Island. He answered; another question was asked, he answered, but then it was my turn so I asked questions—some of the most foolish imaginable, he would look at me and then answer, Crawford was not as bad as Knight because he said he was new, he didn't know. Maurer had the most nerve, start answering and soon be talking about . . . his shipwreck on the island. All in all it has been a great time.

Portrait of Ada Blackjack before she left for the Wrangel Island expedition.
Courtesy of Dartmouth College Library, Rauner Special Collections

Stefansson did not want the truth to get out before they sailed because he didn't want anyone else to steal his idea. He planned to postpone announcing his true reason for the expedition until the men arrived on Wrangel. Then he would state his real objective: claiming for Great Britain the 2,000-square-mile island about 100 miles north of Siberia.

After ownership was established through occupancy, he hoped to get the Canadian government to assume responsibility for the land. Canadian officials had turned down sponsorship of the expedition because of problems Stefansson had had with previous ones. Once the island was in British possession, he believed it could serve as a stop along future polar air routes of dirigibles and airplanes flying from England into China and Japan over the North Pole.

He also believed the island could support a meteorological station to study and forecast northern weather and possibly a radio station. To protect the mission's real purpose, Stefansson let word drift about that the men were involved in a commercial enterprise about which he shared only vague details. To add to the confusion the men caused with their differing answers to questions, the four spread the word that they were going to make their fortunes in trapping for furs. For the most part, however, no one paid much attention to them anyway. Some thought they were searching for gold, but the prevalent belief was that they would never make it to Wrangel Island.

In contrast to the doubters, the young men were so excited about their venture that they wanted to share in the finances as well as in the expedition work itself. Knight wanted to purchase ten shares for $1,000 but had no resources. So he arranged for $50 to be withheld from his salary each month and deposited into an account especially for that purpose. After securing a loan from his brother John, Maurer also purchased ten shares. Crawford bought $500 worth of shares and put $100 down for a two-year option to later buy $1,000 in shares. Since Galle would not receive a salary, he had no money with which to negotiate a purchase.

In addition to his desire to claim Wrangel for the British, Stefansson had a secondary goal for the trip. He hoped to prove his theory that the Arctic was not "a harsh environment that must be fought, but . . . a land that would support a comfortable life for those who adapted their behavior to suit the unique characteristics." He further contended, "There is absolutely nothing heroic in Arctic exploration, for exploration, like any other work, is easily resolved into certain simple rules, which, if properly followed, render it as safe and about as exciting as taxi-driving or a hundred other things which are done in civilization and without a suggestion of heroism either." He believed that white men, properly equipped, could maintain themselves in the Arctic indefinitely.

Such statements made Arctic exploration seem ordinary. But to the four young men, Stefansson pitched the expedition as a grand adventure in a friendly environment with no danger involved. He later told reporters, "The returning party will have a story to tell that will rank with the most romantic in Arctic history."

Ada wasn't sure whether she should even consider the job. She had a paralyzing fear of polar bears, and there were sure to be polar bears in the far north. If one ate her, she would never get back to Bennett. Because of her doubts, she visited a shaman who, in exchange for a little tobacco, foretold her going on the trip but warned of danger and death. He told Ada to especially watch out for knives and fire.

Shamans

Shamans, sometimes called medicine men, were found mostly among native persons, such as Eskimos. Eskimos thought that when a person died, his or her spirit lived on in the spirit world. It was believed that the shaman could control those spirits as well as intercede between them and the people. The shaman covered his face with a large mask, which was believed to possess powers to assist in contacting the spirit world. Bad things happening signaled that the spirits were unhappy. He used charms, music, and ritual objects to interact with the spirits and to discover what the people could do to make the spirits happy again. The shaman might recommend offering gifts, paying a fine for a specific action, or even moving away from the area. Since the money was given to the shaman supposedly to pass on to the spirits, many shamans became quite wealthy.

The shamans also communicated with the spirits to predict the weather, tell the Eskimo hunters where to find game, put a curse on an enemy or evildoer, and predict the future. These beliefs were once held by almost all Eskimos, but today they are rarely followed.

Although the warning scared Ada, she respected the shaman's advice to go on the trip. She was torn between the desire to take care of her son and the need to obtain enough money to get him better medical treatment. Still pondering what to do, Ada went to meet the four men. They assured her that they planned to hire some Eskimo families to accompany them. The husbands would hunt while the women cooked and made or repaired clothing. Ada would live with one of the families.

The men explained that they needed a seamstress because staying warm and dry was essential for the success of their northern adventure. The best way to do that was to have animal skin clothing that was properly made and repaired to protect against the bitter cold winds and the icy waters. The usual Eskimo wardrobe consisted of a fur coat, fur trousers, and skin boots. Only Eskimo women knew how to roll and stitch a seam that was in itself waterproof. On boots they did this by skillfully sewing the soles to the tops with a sinew thread. Arctic clothing sold in stores had an ordinary seam that was greased to make it waterproof. If an Eskimo woman saw someone putting grease on a seam she had constructed, she was insulted, believing her competence was being questioned.

The four men planned to follow Stefansson's advice to hire more than one Eskimo family. They offered Ada and each person in the prospective families a salary of $50 a month for a two-year term, to be deposited directly into a Nome bank while they were on Wrangel. The men believed they had made an agreement with sufficient families for their needs. However, on the day their ship, the *Silver Wave*, got ready to depart Nome for Wrangel Island, the only Eskimo who showed up was 23-year-old Ada Blackjack. Why the others didn't come is not known. Perhaps they feared a trip so far to the north. Perhaps the $50 a month salary seemed too little; Alaska had become more prosperous since the discovery of gold.

The explorers had already hired the ship and paid the deposit to take them to Wrangel, so they didn't have time to seek out more Eskimo families. When Ada saw she was the only Eskimo there, she became suspicious and wanted to go home. She was not sure about being the only woman with four men. But they promised her she would not be alone; they would stop along the way to hire some Eskimo families.

Going so far away from her family scared Ada, and she wanted to stay near Bennett, who was in the children's home. But she was desperate for the money to get him out of the Jesse Lee Home and to provide for his medical needs. She figured that in two years she could save enough to bring him home and perhaps even have enough to take him to a Seattle hospital for special treatment so that he could grow to be strong like other children. For Bennett's sake, Ada decided to go along with the expedition as their seamstress.

The *Silver Wave*, a motor schooner with a gasoline-powered engine, pulled out of the Nome harbor on September 9, 1921. Captain Jack Hammer, an experienced and respected captain, was at the helm. Also aboard the ship was a small gray kitten. The four men had arrived in Nome on the *Victoria*. During their voyage from Seattle the ship's cat produced a litter of kittens, and the chief steward insisted on giving the men the best one as a good luck charm. The men named the little cat Victoria after the ship but soon shortened it to Vic.

On board, Ada stood out from the four white explorers and the crew with her olive skin, straight blue-black hair, and petite size. Under five feet tall and weighing less than 100 pounds, she looked like a child as she stood near the men, watching Nome disappear from view. She seldom spoke to the others, and her dark brown eyes often darted from side to side as if seeking escape.

Before they sailed, the men had given Ada some money for sewing supplies. She bought needles, sinew, linen thread, thimbles, and a recent invention—an Eversharp pencil. It was the first mass-produced pencil that never needed sharpening, and she treasured it. While she shopped for her sewing needs, the men had arranged for their cargo to be loaded.

The expedition was scheduled to last two years, but they were furnished with only enough provisions for six months. The plan was to prove Stefansson's theory about living off the land in the friendly Arctic. Supplies included hunting gear, such as guns and ammunition, fish nets and hooks, and harpoons. Canned or boxed food items, but none in glass, joined the supplies. They did not take much meat or butter because seals, bears, and foxes could provide oil and meat.

Survival items like flashlights, batteries, lanterns, stoves, and cooking gear were added to the goods, along with several tents. They also took basic clothing like socks, mittens, shirts, and underwear, but they limited the amounts

Cats on Ships

Cats and sailors have had a strong bond throughout history. Felines destroy rats and mice that could cause havoc on a ship in various ways: getting into a cargo of grain, chewing on the ship's mooring ropes or woodwork, or carrying diseases. Cats do not like water, but they adapt to travel on it and become companions to lonely sailors.

In 1232, Pope Gregory IX issued a papal edict declaring cats were instruments of the devil. Religious zealots captured cats and threw them into the fires burning witches at the stake. Eventually, such beliefs focused on black cats. However, sailors believe black cats have magical powers that can protect their ships at sea.

They also have many other superstitions about cats. For example, if a cat walks toward a sailor on the deck, it is a sign of good luck. But if the cat turns back, something dire will happen. One popular belief is that cats have magical tails with which they can start storms if they are dissatisfied. Sailors thus strive to keep their cats happy. Even today, felines are valuable members of the crews on many ships.

of outerwear since Ada would provide more fur clothing as needed. To help pass the long days and nights ahead, the men selected 100 secondhand books by a variety of well-known authors. To finish off the supplies, each added favorites, such as gum, candy, tobacco, and chocolate.

Two days after their departure from Nome, they arrived at Russian-held East Cape, Siberia, where they planned to hire some Eskimo families and to purchase an umiak, a light animal-skin boat that can be hauled out of water, dragged across intervening ice floes, and launched again on the other side. These were two essentials that Stefansson had told them they must have. While the ship docked, representatives of the Soviet government boarded the *Silver Wave*. The Russians insisted they be told where the ship was headed and the group's plans.

Authorities laughed when they heard the destination was Wrangel Island. They predicted the explorers would never reach it because of the ice. The young men ignored them because, at that time, there was not a cake of ice visible anywhere. The expedition party's attempts to hire some Eskimo families failed, but, full of confidence, they didn't worry that Ada would have no Eskimo companions or that they would have no hunters to help them. Ada kept her fears to herself and did not share her doubts because she had made a promise, and she didn't break promises.

The men also did not fare well as they tried to buy the umiak. They thought the quoted price of $120 was exorbitant. Knight had enough hunting experience to know that they could catch polar bears, seals, and foxes without a boat. He saw no need to worry about catching walruses.

So the men asked Captain Hammer to sell them his ship's big 700-pound dory, and they didn't purchase the umiak. This was a major mistake; without a proper lightweight boat, they were later on almost powerless in the hunt for walruses, whose meat they would desperately need. But for the time being, they just wanted to start their grand adventure.

The ship encountered a fierce gale from the west not too long after leaving East Cape. The captain and his crew set the sails and the helm to ride out the storm. It subsided, and three days later they came near Wrangel Island. Because of a misty fog, they had little impression of the land that would soon be their home. They later discovered that the kidney-shaped island was made up of three parts, each having its own geographical features. The southern part was a coastal plain with gravel beaches, about nine miles across at its widest point. That gave way to a cluster of two mountain ranges in the middle that on the average rose 1,600 feet above sea level. The northern part was again coastal plains that were 16 miles wide at their broadest point.

The island had no trees but there was plenty of driftwood. During the warmth of its brief summer, rivers flowed to the sea over rolling flat lands whose subsoil was always frozen. Despite the severe climate when access to the island was blocked by ice, Wrangel possessed an abundance of life. As many as 400 polar bears came there in the winter to give birth to their young. Pacific walruses, seals, snow geese, and arctic foxes populated the island, while huge numbers of lemmings and seabirds provided food for the animals.

The men were watching for their destination, Rodgers Harbour, and they spotted it on the evening of September 15. Fighting a heavy surf, they unloaded their cargo and the seven dogs they had purchased in Nome. The men and Ada

Siberian brown lemming on Wrangel Island.
Morales/agefotostock

spent the night on the ship—their last night in real beds for a long time. Ada considered returning to Nome with the *Silver Wave* but later explained: "When we got to Wrangel Island the land looked very large to me, but they said that it was only a small island. I thought at first that I would turn back, but I decided it wouldn't be fair to the boys."

Not sharing Ada's misgivings, the men awoke at about 3:00 AM, and after breakfast, filled with excitement, they erected a flag pole and hoisted the British flag. Having apparently bought into Stefansson's belief that mere occupancy could secure the island for Great Britain, they signed and read aloud a proclamation claiming the island on behalf of King George V.

The proclamation read as follows:

Know by all these presents:

That I, Allan Rudyard Crawford, a native of Canada and a British subject, and three men whose names appear below, members of the Wrangel Island detachment of the Stefansson Arctic Expedition of 1921, on the advice of Counsel of V Stefansson, a British subject, and in consideration of maps of foreign claims, and the occupancy from March 12, 1914, to Sept. 11, 1914, of this island by the survivors of the Brigantine Karluk, Captain R. A. Bartlett, commanding the property of the government of Canada, chartered to operate in the Canadian Arctic expedition of 1913-1918 of which Survivor Chief Engineer Munroe, a native of Scotland and a British subject, raised the British flag and declared this land, known as Wrangel Island, to be the first possession of His Majesty George, King of Great Britain and Ireland, and the dimensions beyond the seas, emperor of India, etc., and a part of the British empire.

Signed & deposited in this monument this 16th day of September, in the year of our Lord 1921.

(Signed)
Allan R. Crawford, commander
E. Lorne Knight, second in command
F. W. Maurer
Milton Galle
Wrangel Island, September 16, 1921.
"God Save the King."

They then sealed the document in a bottle, placed it in a box, and buried it on the island near the place they had landed.

Knight had started keeping a diary while on the *Silver Wave*, and he now noted the expedition's only drawback at that time was the unhealthy condition of the seven sled dogs they had brought with them from Nome. The dogs were "in rather poor shape, but will do my best to get them in good condition when we reach the island. The season is getting late and a good many things must be done before the freezeup, so we are anxious to get started with our work."

Captain Hammer and his crew left behind the ship's dory, the five members of the expedition, the dogs, and the cat. The Wrangel party would not see anyone else until the next summer when another ship was scheduled to bring them needed supplies.

Meet Vilhjalmur Stefansson

The parents of William Stephenson, who later changed his name to Vilhjalmur Stefansson to reflect his Icelandic heritage, were among 250 colonists who came to Canada to escape the deplorable economic conditions in Iceland during the late 19th century. They called the settlement "New Iceland." However, soon after the birth of William on November 3, 1879, the Stephensons moved to North Dakota, where the boy spent his childhood and youth.

William had a brilliant mind that allowed him, despite a lack of previous formal education, to enter the University of North Dakota at the age of 18. He stayed at the university until his junior year when excessive absences caused his expulsion. The tall, slim, blue-eyed blond next transferred to the University of Iowa, where in one year he gained enough credits by examination to earn his degree.

Stefansson then headed to Harvard University to study folklore and anthropology, the comparison of human societies and cultures. During the summer breaks of 1904 and

1905, he traveled to Iceland to study the relationship of the people's diet to their health. After serving as a teaching assistant at Harvard during the regular term, he left that university to engage in Arctic exploration, eventually going on three expeditions, lasting from 18 months to five years.

In 1906 he agreed to join the Leffingwell-Mikkelsen expedition as their ethnologist, which meant he would study the characteristics and relationships of the Eskimos on the Mackenzie River in Canada. Stefansson planned to meet the expedition's sponsors on Herschel Island, but when he arrived, they had not come. He later learned they had lost their ship when it became trapped in ice. Stefansson was left to make his own way to the Mackenzie River. He stayed in the area for 18 months, spending time with the Eskimos (Inuits) to learn more about their ways.

While on Herschel Island, he had heard an intriguing story from a whaler spending the winter there. Captain "Charlie" Klengenberg told Stefansson about a group of natives he claimed to have met. He stated that these people had never seen a man with white skin before but that many of them had blue eyes and blond hair. He supported his story by showing Stefansson some knives and tools made by the natives out of copper. Stefansson decided to launch another expedition to determine if the Copper Inuits, as he dubbed them, really existed.

However, 28-year-old Stefansson had difficulty obtaining funds for a trip north. He finally secured enough money from the Canadian government and some private institutions to set out. From 1908 to 1912, Stefansson led his own expedition to the Arctic. They explored Alaska and the Canadian archipelago, a group of 94 major islands and more than 30,000 minor islands north of the Canadian mainland. During this foray he discovered four more islands of the archipelago—Borden, Brock, Meighen, and Lougheed. The trip also led to his meeting the Copper Eskimos, or Inuits, on Victoria Island.

Stefansson wrote a letter to one of his expedition sponsors: "West of the Coppermine [River on Victoria Island] we found over 200 people who had never seen a white man, whose ancestors had never seen one, who knew of no past relations with people to the west, and whose territory was supposed by geographers to be definitely known to be uninhabited." Yet many of them had blond hair and blue eyes. In addition, they had a stouter, heavier build than other Eskimos, resembling the muscular build of whalers on fishing boats. Just as Captain Klengenberg had described, these Inuits used tools and utensils made of copper.

While Stefansson stayed with the Copper Inuits, he needed an interpreter. He hired Fanny Pannigabluk, a native woman, to travel with the expedition. The two became close, and their son, Alik Alahuk, or Alex, was born on March 10, 1910. Stefansson left them both behind when he finished his study of the Copper Inuits. Although the couple's relationship was well known among her people, Stefansson never discussed the woman or his son with others.

From 1913 to 1918 Stefansson headed a Canadian government-sponsored expedition to the Arctic. He told the government that the purpose was to determine whether

The Karluk *Tragedy*

Captain Bob Bartlett feared the *Karluk*, an old whaling ship, was not strong enough to plow through icy waters as part of the Canadian Arctic Expedition led by Vilhjalmur Stefansson. Despite Bartlett's concerns, the *Karluk* set out from Esquimalt, British Columbia, on June 17, 1913, to make scientific explorations along the northern coast of Canada and to look for new land in the uncharted seas north and northwest of Alaska. By August 15 the ship had become trapped in an ice pack in the Bering Strait.

For five months the ship remained stuck, along with 20 crew members and scientists, two Eskimo men, and one Eskimo woman with her two little daughters. Gradually, the *Karluk* drifted to the northwest with ice floes pressuring it on all sides. One day it split apart with a sharp, cracking noise and a mighty trembling. Water poured into the ship as Captain Bartlett and his crew rushed to unload their supplies on the ice pack before the ship disappeared into a narrow hole.

Everyone managed to get off the ship, but they were marooned on the shifting ice. In a 100-mile struggle across the ice floes to reach land, eleven men died or disappeared. The survivors finally reached Wrangel Island, where they were stranded for another six months before their rescue.

there was an undiscovered continent at the top of the world. Privately, he also wanted to test his theory of the "friendly Arctic." He believed that rather than being a remote, icy place filled with potential dangers, the Arctic was a place where white men could live off the land if they followed the Eskimos' ways.

Finalizing arrangements for the Canadian expedition had not been easy. There had been difficulties in obtaining sufficient funding because Stefansson's reputation had been marred by the sinking of the *Karluk* in a previous exploration. When the ship became locked in ice but before it sank in icy waters, he had left. The impatient Stefansson, unable to tolerate inactivity, took three other white men, two Eskimo hunters, and the best dogs to find caribou to get fresh meat to prevent scurvy developing in the crew. When they returned after a few days, they found the *Karluk* had drifted away and was no longer in sight. Stefansson did not worry about those aboard the ship because he knew they could use umiaks to reach shore. He did not appear to consider what would happen after that. Stefansson and the other men then made their way over 300 miles of ice and snow to Point Barrow, the northernmost part of the United States. He wrote a telegram about the *Karluk*'s disappearance and gave the message to an Eskimo to take to Nome 400 miles away.

From there Stefansson went to Herschel Island, where another of his expedition ships, the *Belvedere*, waited with supplies. He outfitted a dog sled expedition to explore uncharted lands that he believed lay to the north. He named two men, Storkerson and Anderson, both experienced Arctic explorers, as leaders of a Northern and a Southern group. Stefansson joined the Northern party. They had one sled, six dogs, and a minimal number of supplies when they set out across the ice to explore around the Beaufort Sea. They planned to live off the land when their supplies were gone.

For the next four years the Canadian government did not know where Stefansson was. Most assumed he had died. When he reappeared, he seemed strong and healthy, apparently having proved his theory about living off the land in the friendly Arctic. However, the fact that he had left the *Karluk* trapped in ice affected his attempt to obtain funds for the Wrangel Island expedition. The decision to leave the ship was one that haunted Stefansson the rest of his life as opponents claimed he had deserted his expedition members. Stefansson was finally able to get back to the Arctic in spring 1918, when he was picked up by Captain Lane and the *Teddy Bear* at Cape Kellett, Canada.

At age 39 Stefansson entered the second phase of his life. He capitalized on the discovery of the four archipelago islands to add to his reputation as an explorer. This led to his becoming a popular lecturer, who fascinated audiences with his ability to spin a story that he illustrated with his own hand-colored lantern slides. He joined the Chautauqua lecture circuit, and he wrote over two dozen books plus hundreds of pamphlets and articles. He acquired a following of young men who were eager to assist at lectures by introducing him, managing his lantern slides, and even serving as his secretary. Three of those young men—Lorne Knight, Frederick Maurer, and Milton Galle—carried out his next expedition.

Circuit Chautauqua

Circuit Chautauqua began in 1874 as an adult education movement that focused on training Sunday school teachers. Named after New York's Chautauqua Lake, where the first session was held, the Chautauqua assemblies grew and spread throughout rural America until the mid-1920s. Gradually, education and entertainment became combined in the form of lectures, concerts, and plays, usually as part of traveling groups that often stopped near small towns to set up their big brown tents. These traveling groups became known as the "Circuit Chautauqua." At the circuit's peak, over 10,000 communities in 45 states with audiences up to 45 million participated in a Circuit Chautauqua.

Depending upon who arranged a particular program, presenters ranged from animal acts to vaudeville to Shakespearean actors to lecturers who provided educational opportunities for adults. Every topic from current events to travel to humorous tales could be heard. Music was also a part of the traveling shows, with bands being especially popular. Vocalists ranged from opera singers to Jubilee Singers who sang African American spirituals. Small towns welcomed the Circuit Chautauqua each summer until the Great Depression brought about the gradual end to most of the traveling shows.

Stefansson was a popular lecturer on the Circuit Chautauqua, and his stories of Arctic life fascinated crowds, especially in the small towns of rural America. In one 21-day period, he delivered 23 lectures in California, Nevada, and Utah. His book *The Friendly Arctic* brought new light to people's knowledge about the Eskimos and became his best-loved book. But Stefansson was a visionary; while he lectured on the circuit, he still wanted to explore other lands. He decided to send four young men to Wrangel Island to do the actual exploratory work for him while he continued his public presentations and other writings.

From 1936 to 1945 Stefansson served as an adviser on polar flights for Pan-American Airways. During World War II he performed similar services for the US military. In 1940, at the age of 62, Stefansson married a 28-year-old staff member, Evelyn Schwartz Baird. For the next 10 years they divided their time between New York and a farm they had purchased in Vermont. He continued correspondence with people on both sides of the Atlantic, including Orville Wright and Sir Arthur Conan Doyle. He kept every piece of paper he received and made carbon copies of letters he wrote.

He had such an accumulation of papers and books that he rented a second house just to store them all. At the end of the decade, Stefansson donated his massive collection of polar materials to Dartmouth College in New Hampshire. He became an Arctic consultant for the school, and his wife became the first librarian of the Stefansson Collection. The couple remained at Dartmouth until Stefansson died of a stroke at the age of 82 on August 26, 1962. He had just completed his autobiography, *Discovery*.

2

SETTLING ON THE ISLAND

THE FOUR WRANGEL ISLAND expedition members had been so eager to claim the island for Great Britain that they planted the British flag and read the proclamation before the *Silver Wave* left. This was a tactical error because the crew members, all Americans, saw the Union Jack raised on the island and felt they had been duped. They realized they could have planted a US flag and claimed the island for their own country.

The *Silver Wave* headed back to Nome, where they reported what they considered a trick. Although there were mutterings among US government leaders, no action was taken. Stefansson ignored any other claims to the island, arguing that international law did not recognize ownership of property that had been left unoccupied for five years. At that time, no one argued with him.

In a letter to Stefansson conveyed on the returning *Silver Wave*, Crawford assured their sponsor they had been very quiet about their mission because the Russians at East Cape seemed to think they owned the island. He described the team's arrival and initial impressions of Wrangel Island:

> Dear Mr. Stefansson: Commencing this letter ½ mi. offshore. Left Nome Sept. 9th. Called East Cape, Siberia, to purchase skin boat. Sighted island noon yesterday. Resembles in outline and color country round Lewiston, Idaho. Large flat spaces near coast but seems to be mostly hilly. Snow on highest of hills looks like this year's. Have as yet seen not a single ice cake. . . At present we are one mi. west Rodger's Harbour. Fox and bear tracks abundant . . . Everyone seems contented.

In his diary, Knight praised the island's natural beauty: "A beautiful day. Maurer, Galle, and I cut and stacked wood all day, in preparation for hauling on the arrival of snow. Crawford built grub boxes, and a tool chest. Saw a seal, and dozens of seagulls and terns. The gulls are all flying west, no doubt turning south at some point further on. The surf is still running rather heavy, and no ice in sight."

The men wanted to take advantage of the late summer temperatures that were still above freezing and the dry weather before September storms began. The next few days were spent building tents and setting up camp about four miles east of Doubtful Harbour. Knight recorded their activities in his diary:

September 20: Busy digging out the side of a cut bank for space to pitch our winter quarters. We can use one side of the bank for a side of the house and the roof will be sod. We will pitch the 10 x 12 and the 8 y 10 tents end to end (inside the house) and will use the small tent for a kitchen and the large tent for living quarters.

The kitchen tent also provided sleeping accommodations for Ada.

They placed the several wood-burning stoves they had brought with them in such a way that the stovepipes were tall enough to reach through the roof of the snow house when the snow blocks were built around the tents. The pipes also had to be high enough to clear the tent's ridge poles by one or two feet in order to prevent wind from blowing the smoke down into the stovepipe and back into the house.

The men paid little attention to Ada while they prepared the camp and got their tools and meteorological equipment ready for their scientific experiments. Ada was in an unconventional situation—the only woman living with four men. None of them seemed to care what effect this vast wilderness would have on a young woman raised in a city. They were determined to have a grand adventure. Since they did not yet need what she could provide—new fur clothing—they ignored her and went about setting up their camp. Lorne Knight seldom mentioned her in his diary and even if he did, the remarks were brief and factual: she was "sewing clothing, and . . . doing very nicely."

The shy, petite woman was likely overwhelmed by the vast, unpopulated expanse. She had had training for household work, not for living in a wilderness. She liked nice clothes and hats. Now all she had were thick, bulky fur clothes. She surely missed Bennett, whose medical needs had motivated her to accept the job in the first place. She probably felt that the men had betrayed her, promising to hire at least one Eskimo family with whom she could have a relationship. Ada had been on Wrangel Island only a short time when she began to brood about her situation.

Alone with her thoughts, Ada sewed clothing from the skins the team had brought with them while the men got acquainted with the island's resources. On the 25th they

One of hundreds of polar bears that inhabit Wrangel Island.
Superstock

erected a 40-foot permanent flag pole and raised the Union Jack. As a scientific experiment, they preserved the skin of an owl. After Maurer shot at their first bear, Knight took a shot. Although he hit the animal, it continued to come after him. Knight sat down, braced his gun, and took careful aim, shooting the bear in the head and killing him instantly about 100 yards from their camp. The bear was only three-fourths grown with poor fur and medium fat. At the time this was not a problem because there was no shortage of game. Every time the men took a walk, they saw bears.

None of them had any idea how poorly they were equipped for the months ahead. They didn't believe what they had been told about the ice because no ice dotted the ocean around the island. All they saw were foamy breakers rolling onto the beaches. The ice was so late in coming it was not surprising that they felt the warnings exaggerated. They did not realize the unusual nature of the weather that year.

The men hauled wood and constructed a frame for a house in preparation to insert snow blocks when snow came. Ada fastened hoods onto the reindeer-skin coats they had brought with them because the men needed them in the extreme cold. With that task finished, she began to sew other clothing. They followed this routine for about two weeks. Then the trouble started.

Left alone with her sewing, Ada grew ever more homesick and developed a crush on Crawford. With his green eyes, dark hair parted in the middle, neatly trimmed moustache, and tall, lanky physique, Crawford had caught her attention as they made their way from Nome to the island. He was somewhat shy, a trait he shared with Ada. He was also polite and respectful when he spoke to her. Ada spent time near him whenever she could and cast frequent admiring glances his way. On occasion she brought him choice bits of food she had prepared. The other men mocked her infatuation.

One day near the end of September, at about two o'clock in the afternoon, Ada left the four men behind and went out of the tent. For her to leave the safety of the camp and take a chance on meeting a dreaded polar bear showed how desperate she felt. She did not return within the hour, and Crawford became anxious. When he walked out of the tent, he noticed a box nearby. When he opened it, he found a note, Ada's prized Eversharp pencil, and a finger ring. The note instructed Crawford to keep the ring and the pencil to remember her.

There were tracks, so Crawford and Knight followed them inland toward the hills. After about an hour of fast walking, they saw Ada. When she spotted the men, she screamed and ran from them. Out of her clothes dropped a half-full bottle of liniment, an oily lotion used to relieve pain. When she saw the men following her, she drank the liniment to poison herself because she feared big, boisterous Lorne Knight. Earlier that day, she had seen him sharpening a knife and remembered the shaman's warning about knives. She thought Knight was going to kill her. Ada returned to camp, sick from the ointment she had swallowed, and begging Crawford for protection from the others.

Whenever the men went out for walks, they would encounter several bears but they didn't collect much meat. Sometime in October, Knight wrote: "This morning Galle went eastward to the three bears killed, intending to bring back a ham from one of the cubs, but he returned with the information that the cubs had been nearly all eaten by the foxes." Galle leaving the carcasses of the bears behind after hunting them was not uncommon for the men. They often did so while they waited for enough snow to fall that their sled could more easily transport the heavy meat back to camp.

Numerous bears were not afraid to approach the camp, as Knight's diary indicated: "Eight bears were seen today and literally hundreds of tracks." Apparently believing that there would always be bears to kill for food, they made no efforts to preserve extra meat.

A bigger problem than bears was Ada's strange behavior. Knight noted in his diary that she seemed more like a child of 8 or 10 than a mature woman. On October 3 he wrote:

The woman has had several crying spells to-day and tells us that she was warned in Nome by a fortune teller who told her to be careful of fire and knives. We all have a great deal of use for knives and she, seeing us use them and believing the fiction told her by the fortune teller, is frightened stiff. A few minutes ago she asked me to get my rifle ready and when she sleeps to kill her. In the next breath she asks us to save her life and not let anyone harm her.

This happens half a dozen times a day . . . We treat her as nice as can be. One minute her spells look like sham and the next minute real.

Arctic Hysteria

First noted in 1892, Arctic hysteria has long been debated as to whether it is a real mental condition. It mostly affected Eskimo women and was believed to be caused by the dark, harsh winters in the far North. In earlier times, Eskimos believed evil spirits possessed the women.

Known victims of Arctic hysteria displayed similar behaviors. Prior to an attack, they either withdrew from others or became very irritable. Then a bizarre tantrum began: they headed outdoors despite temperatures below freezing, tore off their clothing, and ran around naked, shouting meaningless words. These actions lasted from 30 minutes to 2 hours and were often followed by up to 12 hours of seizures and coma. The individual awoke with no memory of the odd behaviors.

Other possible things thought to be the cause of Arctic hysteria, besides the long, dark winters, included an excess of vitamin A found in their diet of polar bear liver, advanced hypothermia, calcium deficiency, or a cry for attention.

Initially the men tried coaxing Ada to be calm. When that didn't work, they became sterner with her. But the hysterical episodes continued for several days. Then, with no explanation, Ada resumed her sewing and asked Crawford for a religious book. Knight gave her his grandfather's prayer book. She read it, and peace reigned throughout most of October, as an entry in Knight's diary showed: "All we need now is snow for the walls and roof. Our seamstress is working diligently, and has our winter boots about finished." But later in October, she quit working again and refused to give a reason for doing so.

The men spent all of October 22 moving into their winter house. Enough snow had fallen and frozen that they were able to cut snow blocks and cover the frame house and the two tents. The completed house was 14 feet wide

Placing snow blocks around tents for winter protection.
Courtesy of Dartmouth College Library, Rauner Special Collections

and 24 feet long with an additional 9-by-14 foot storm shed in front. They spent the next several days improving their quarters until they were satisfied with their comfort. They also moved their supplies into the storm shed, which not only kept the wood dry but protected the front tent door from swirling snow when it was opened.

Crawford built a table for the kitchen, and Maurer made the door for the front tent. Then on the last day of the month, they retrieved some bear meat they had cached, waiting for the snow. Knight wrote, "All hands went with a sled and dogs to our two caches of bear meat to the westward. The large bear and cub killed by Galle and Maurer were all eaten by birds and foxes. The first bear killed by Maurer and me had all been packed [transported on backs of men or dogs] home excepting the head and neck, which we now brought. Also hauled some wood to camp."

Then in early November Ada disappeared for several days. The men could not see that she had taken any food with her, but they thought she took a nightgown and some underwear. The weather was bad, with drifting snow. When Ada had not returned by the third day, Knight and Crawford hitched the dogs to a sled and followed some tracks that Galle had noticed. Just an hour later in the distance they spotted a dark form. It was Ada, walking toward the camp and wearing her usual camp clothing with a Siberian native reindeer suit over that. Under the outer garments were underwear and a nightgown. At a distance she looked like an inverted sack of potatoes.

The men bundled her on the sled and took her back to camp, where she refused to talk. Although they punished her for running away by denying her any food except hard bread and water, they knew that while they were away from camp, she ate whatever she wanted. Knight wrote in his diary: "This may sound funny to the reader, but I can assure him that it is not funny to the four of us to have a foolish female howling and refusing to work and eating all our good grub." The men neglected to include Ada in their conversations and in their planning, and so she had no way of knowing what each day would bring.

By this time, Crawford had explored much of the island, and on November 3 he and Galle, each with a backpack, set out to climb a large mountain north of their camp. Crawford planned to do some geological work. However, they returned that same night because of fierce winds that blew across the island.

Prior to their departure from Nome, the men had received instructions from Stefansson regarding campsites. In mid-November they changed their living arrangements according to what he had told them. They established a second camp at Rodgers Harbour, eight miles east of the main camp at Doubtful Harbour. Crawford and Maurer moved there. Ada and the other two men remained behind. Crawford and Maurer planned to use their camp as a base for trapping operations. Knight and Galle would cover the traps in the vicinity nearest them.

The eight-mile separation of the two camps did not keep the four from visiting one another frequently. Ada still feared Knight, and with only the two men remaining with her, she became friends with Galle. He treated her like an equal and called her by name instead of using "the woman" as the others did. They told each other stories from their cultures. She liked Jack and the Beanstalk, especially the magic beans, and he enjoyed the Eskimo legends told to her in childhood. With him she could laugh.

Throughout November, Ada alternated between doing some work and not doing anything. Her refusal to sew worried the men, who didn't know how to make their own clothing. When Knight asked her one day if she had come on the expedition hoping to marry one of them, she admitted that she had. Her preference was Crawford; she had decided that Galle was more like a younger brother. Knight did not comment.

The next morning Ada took a lantern and went to the alternate trapping camp to see Crawford and Maurer. A short time later, Knight realized she was missing and followed her tracks. When he caught up with her, she was standing outside the men's tent because they refused to allow her inside. Knight decided not to take her back on the sled and told her she would have to either walk back or sleep outside as she had been warned not to leave the main camp. She arrived exhausted at the main camp about 7:30 PM. The next morning when she refused to patch a pair of boots, Knight decided to try another tactic. He tied her to the flagpole until she agreed to mend them. This seems harsh punishment for someone who may have been suffering from Arctic hysteria.

After only two months on the island, the group ran out of fresh meat. Up to that point, game had been plentiful—seals, foxes, and polar bears. Because of insufficient snow on which to pull carcasses on a sled, they had not preserved

Pacific walruses resting on ice floe on Wrangel Island.
Morales/age fotostock

most of their catches. With so much available meat when they first arrived, they became lackadaisical about hunting and preserving meat for a time when hunting may not be as good.

However, diary entries showed no concern about the lack of food. They believed that the supply ship would be there in a few months, so they ate the food supplies they had brought with them. They even shared their food with the dogs. Knight's diary revealed that he was feeding the dogs cracklings (crispy, fried pork skins) brought from Nome. When the cracklings were almost gone, he cooked rotten potatoes mixed with a few crumbs for the animals.

Walruses were still available, but the men couldn't hunt for the big animals because they didn't have an umiak to navigate between the floating ice cakes. The heavy dory was useless in trying to move in those waters. The men stood on the beach and looked at the tons of food just out of reach.

The days stretched out in a boring monotony as Knight noted: "Supper is over and there is not a great deal to do so I will write a little. Galle caught a fox today, the first one so far. Maurer and Galle are shaking dice for chewing gum. Crawford is reading. I am tired of reading, hence this spurt of mine. I have just finished building a sled for hauling wood so will hit the hay and get up early and spend the day with our excellent bow-wows." There is no mention of Ada or what she did on these boring days.

The men hoped to kill another polar bear because they knew they could last a year on polar bear and seal meat plus the food brought with them. They finally killed a full-grown male with a good skin. However, the warm weather prevented any snow, and they could not move the sled on dry land. They cut up the carcass, saved a little meat for the dogs, and then stored the rest of the meat under piles of stones. By the time they returned to retrieve the meat, foxes and other bears had eaten most of it.

Then all at once they had an excess of potential meat. With the arrival of so many pregnant bears seeking dens during the winter months, they could not conceive of a future time when there would be a shortage of bear steaks or dog food. They did not kill as many as they should have because moving the carcasses on the sled over bare ground was still impossible. Then they lost one of their best dogs. Snowball went crazy—he started fighting with the other dogs and snapping at the men. He refused to eat and would not stop barking. No one knew what to do for him, and finally he died.

The dog's death reminded the men they had not provided any shelter for the animals while building their own snow house. Although they were well-furred Eskimo dogs, the animals needed protection from the gale force storms that blew over the island. The men built a house with an alcove for each of the dogs. They connected it to their own house so that heat could pass from one to the other.

Before he set out on his tasks on November 24, Knight told Ada to make some skin socks and mittens and to start scraping a deer skin. Scraping was a preliminary step to get the skin soft for sewing. When he came back later that day, Ada was gone. Knight completed a delivery of supplies to the trapping camp and returned to the main camp. Ada had just come back. She said she had been out walking on the ice and had followed a fox's trail.

A common Eskimo belief was that certain spirits lived in hollows in hills and came out in the guise of foxes. By following their trails, the tracker could find the foxes' habitat, where the human would be treated pleasantly. Sometimes the Eskimo married one of the hill people. Ada wanted to find these people because she believed they would be kind to her.

As the December days passed, bears became less plentiful but more inquisitive. On Christmas Eve, Knight took a sled and went to the trapping camp to get Crawford and Maurer to bring them back to the main camp to share in the holiday. When he reached the men, he discovered that about an hour before his arrival the two had had a close call with a hungry invader.

The quarters at the trapping camp were an 8-by-10 tent stretched inside a snow house and in front of that a 4-by-8 storm shed. The front door, about four feet high and 16 inches wide, was the only entrance into the tent. That morning the two men were eating breakfast when Maurer decided to raise the tent flap to look for something in the storage shed. There in front of him was a huge polar bear with its big head stuck in the door. Maurer gave a loud shout, but the bear ignored him.

Their rifles were all outside. Because they had no way to get to their weapons, the two men retreated to the back of the tent. All of a sudden, the bear apparently smelled something that appealed to it and tried to enter the tent. Fortunately, its shoulders were too broad to get through the door. Crawford and Maurer threw firewood, pots and pans, and finally their dishes at the huge animal. Although they hit the bear several times, he was determined to get to the food he smelled. He moved his snout from side to side while gastric juices dripped from the end of his tongue. At last, they threw pieces of burning wood from the stove, and the bear retreated a short distance.

Crawford, who was dressed more warmly than Maurer, rushed out of the tent to grab his gun. By that time the bear was about 100 yards away. Maurer followed Crawford, dropped to the ground, and took aim. He pulled the trigger, but the cartridge did not explode. It had frozen while the rifles were outside. When the bear started to move away, Maurer followed it a short distance, but by that time the bear was going too fast to overtake it.

When Knight got back to the main camp, he discovered that Galle, after returning from checking the traps, found a large polar bear sniffing around the main camp. There was

Nanook, the Polar Bear

Eskimos believed the polar bear, or Nanook, had intense power in both the natural and spirit worlds. Therefore, bear spirits must be respected at all times. According to legend, polar bears could turn into humans after removing their bear skins. In human form, the bear could use weapons to capture and eat the Eskimo. Such beliefs led to rituals that were followed when the Eskimo killed a bear. For example, the hunter who brought in the catch must remove his outer clothes before he came into the igloo, similar to the bear's removing its skin once inside its den.

At times Nanook was kind. There were many stories about Eskimos saved from starvation by a polar bear that either caught seals for the humans or allowed itself to be killed for food. In that case, after the Eskimos killed the bear, they recognized its soul by hanging its skins in an honored place in their igloo.

Nanook's spirit then reappeared in another bear that was willing to make a similar sacrifice of its life. However, if the Eskimos did not pay proper respect, the spirit reappeared as a demon and took revenge on the disrespectful hunters.

no sign of Ada. With one perfect shot, Galle killed the bear and then went in search of the woman, fearing the bear had harmed her. He found Ada in the tent in the dark, paralyzed with fear. Apparently the bear had been outside the tent for a while. She had been so frightened when she saw it that she failed to add wood to the fire and consequently the fire had gone out. She was almost frozen, both physically and emotionally.

Meet Milton Galle

Milton Robert Harvey Galle, at 19 the youngest member of the Wrangel Island expedition, was born on March 6, 1902, in New Braunfels, Texas. He attended school there, graduating from the New Braunfels Public School that housed all grades from kindergarten through high school. He was the son of Harry and Alma Galle and brother to Alfred Emil and Elsie Marie Augusta. The Galle family traced its roots to Émile Gallé, one of the masters of French glass in Alsace-Lorraine. In 1914, 10 years after Émile's death, Milton's father received an $8,000 inheritance from the glassmaking factory. He used the money to build the Galle home in New Braunfels.

If it had not been for the Circuit Chautauqua coming to New Braunfels, Milton Galle would probably have never become an Arctic explorer. The arrival of the traveling show was a huge event. The varied entertainments lasted for a week, with both day and evening shows. Milton attended every day. After he heard Vilhjalmur Stefansson give a presentation about his Arctic adventures, the teenager was hooked. He decided that he wanted to be an Arctic explorer too.

In 1919 he applied for a job with the Circuit Chautauqua and was assigned to run the projector during Stefansson's lectures. As they traveled across the country from April to August, Galle and Stefansson got to know each other well. Milton had grown up in a household that spoke several languages, and Stefansson saw that Milton's fluency in Spanish, German, and English was a benefit as they traveled to different locales. Everywhere they went, people were drawn to Milton's lanky stature and his quick grin. After a few months, Stefansson invited Milton to serve as his secretary. In that role he became acquainted with Lorne Knight and Frederick Maurer, who were also working for the Circuit Chautauqua. He listened with avid attention to their stories about the Arctic adventures the two had already had. These tales convinced Milton even more that he wanted to join Stefansson's next expedition.

In August 1921, on his prized Corona typewriter, Milton wrote a long letter to his family expressing his joy in having been selected as one of the four young men to go on the Wrangel Island expedition: "By now you have, I'm sure heared [sic] that I am one of those four lucky ones that are going north on STEFANSSON'S expedition. I am simply overjoyed, yes tickeled [sic] to death."

Milton's mother was not overjoyed about the letter's contents and expressed concern to her son. From California, he sent her a telegram that concluded, "To my thinking it is about time I leave the apron behind." Perhaps hoping to

Gallé Glass

French glassmaker Émile Gallé pioneered certain innovative techniques in the glassmaking industry during the Art Nouveau period. Early examples of the glass were clear or lightly tinted, decorated with enamel and engraving. Deeply colored, almost opaque glass, often layered, was next. Plant designs, including leaves, flowers, vines, and fruits, were carved or etched into the multiple layers. The next step added characteristics of Japanese art. Later versions had a verse of poetry embedded in each piece, causing it to be referred to as "poetry in glass." The glass received a grand prize at the Paris Exhibition of 1878. This recognition led to the Gallés building their own factory, where they could experiment with glassmaking possibilities and create original designs.

The factory eventually employed 300 people to meet the unprecedented demand for Gallé glass. This resulted in the creation of industrial techniques that enabled the glass to be mass produced. Even then, new techniques, such as applying metallic foils between colored glass sheets, delighted glass collectors. Production of the glass ceased in 1936, and today it can be found only in antique shops and in museum collections.

appease her, he sent her flowers on Mother's Day, a gesture noted in the New Braunfels newspaper. After providing his parents with the details he had about the expedition, Milton promised to write again from Nome, Alaska, the last stop before leaving for Wrangel Island. The fact that Stefansson told Galle he could not afford to pay him a salary did not seem to dim the young man's enthusiasm. His only hope for income would be the furs that he collected from animals he killed.

Milton's parents wanted to meet the man who was sending their son into an unknown territory. When they heard that Stefansson might be lecturing in San Marcos, Texas, they wrote a letter inviting him to visit with them in nearby New Braunfels so that they could all get to know one another better. From Nome, Milton also wrote a letter to Stefansson encouraging him to meet his family. Stefansson finally answered the invitation and stated that he would not be in Texas any time in the near future.

The Galles' invitation was the beginning of frequent letters between the Galles and Stefansson. These queries to gain information about the expedition increased after the Galles received word a year later that the *Teddy Bear* had not been able to reach Wrangel with its load of replacement supplies and that consequently there was no mail from their son.

3

CHANGING WINDS

ADA'S DEEP-SEATED FEAR of polar bears was not unusual for Eskimos at that time. They thought that all objects possessed a spirit—either good or bad. Eskimos wanted the polar bear spirits to look kindly upon them, so they strove not to annoy or anger them.

There were many legends and myths that caused their fears. A popular one with Eskimo children resembled the story of Goldilocks and the Three Bears. According to the ancient tale, a young woman visited the house next door, planning to welcome her new neighbors. She did not know that they were polar bears disguised as humans.

The next-door family was not at home when she arrived. She peeked in the windows and decided to wait for them inside. She wandered around their house until the door opened and, instead of the humans she had seen earlier, polar bears entered. Frightened, she ran to hide. From her hiding place she saw the bears drop their skins on the floor and resume their human appearance. Then they sniffed the air and said, *"Inuksunirjualinnaa Maanangat!"* which translates as, "I smell a human in here." The woman trembled in fear as she hid. All the next day she waited for the bears to leave the house. Finally, they did and she returned home. But forever after she feared all neighbors were polar bears in disguise, just waiting to eat her. Because Ada had heard stories like this so many times, she shared the same fear.

Ada also continued to be lonely, and her strange behavior returned on December 16. When Galle came back from checking his traps, he found that Ada had packed her two suitcases. A short time later she disappeared for a while and then returned without them. Instead she had a pack on her back into which she had apparently placed some items. She must have hidden the suitcases inland somewhere. Back at the camp, she gave no explanation for her actions but went to get herself some dried fruit and hard bread.

This time the men refused to let her stay in the tent until she promised to sew again. They told her she had to live in the old snow house until she started sewing. Since the weather was warm and calm, no harm could come to her there. The next day she asked Knight what he wanted her to sew and got to work.

The seamstress's attitude became happier as Christmas approached. She worked hard to prepare food for a small celebration. For several days in a row, Knight noted in his diary that Ada was very industrious and happy, especially after she learned Crawford and Maurer would join them for the holiday: "December 21, 1921: Blowing a strong gale from the west, so did not go out today. The woman is working like a Trojan and rose this morning at 6 o'clock to bake bread. The dogs are inside and comfortable. Nothing to do until the blow is over." He had similar short entries on Christmas Eve: "December 24, 1921: Galle is working on a wind gauge. The woman is baking, cooking, washing dishes and sewing." And again on Christmas Day: "December 25, 1921: Spending the day doing nothing but eating, although we are not hungry. Potatoes a la O'Brien, cake, bread and butter, coffee. We finished up the evening playing poker for smokes. Clear, light breeze from north."

After Christmas the days dragged for the men. Although they told jokes, read, and played solitaire to pass the time, the humdrum routine bored them. To add to their problems, another dog died. Knight noted in his diary: "I went out to look at the dogs and found one of them dead. We hauled wood (yesterday) and at one time I thought I saw him stagger slightly, but, as he seemed to be working well later, I paid no attention to it. When I fed him he was apparently all right. He was one of our best dogs and . . . his loss will be greatly felt." In the Arctic the loss of a dog was like the loss of a friend.

With one fewer dogs, the men decided that it would be more practical to all live together. Crawford and Maurer had caught only one fox in the time they lived at the alternate site. They decided to abandon that camp for a while because living in one place would make it easier for the dogs. The animals would not have to haul as much wood for heating and cooking if the five people lived together.

Huskies with dog sled.
Image Source

Knight recorded in his diary that January 18, 1922, was a day of bad luck. After breakfast, Crawford and Maurer had gone east to a lead, a channel of water in the ice, to catch a seal. However, they forgot to take the retriever with them.

Shortly after the other two left to go seal hunting, Knight and Galle realized Crawford and Maurer had left the retriever behind. They decided to take it to them. When the two were about a half mile from the others, Crawford shot a seal, which then started to drift east. There was no way to get within 100 yards of the animal because of the water. All they could do was hope the current would change, but it didn't. Maurer shot another seal about 75 feet from the edge of the firm ice, and this time Knight used the retriever to pull the animal to the edge of the slush ice about 30 feet away.

They worked until dark trying to grab hold of the seal but it disappeared when its body became detached from the retriever. This was another occasion when the umiak would have allowed them to maneuver between the ice cakes, capture the seal, and fill their larder with seal meat and blubber.

Another day later in the month proved to be luckier. They shot a mother polar bear and her cub, breaking up

Retriever

A retriever, also called an *ilhook*, is an Eskimo device for retrieving seals killed in open water out of reach of the hunter. The tool is made from a piece of wood and shaped into a float about the size and shape of an elongated lightbulb. Curved metal hooks protrude from the wood. A long rawhide line is also securely fastened to the float.

The hunter whirls the float rapidly around his head and then lets it fly out past the seal, carrying the line with it. If the float doesn't fall on the seal, the hunter moves along the shore or the ice until the float is in such a position that it can be pulled directly across the animal. The metal barbs then snag the seal and hold it while the animal is dragged ashore or onto the ice.

the food monotony by providing them with fresh meat. They found the cub meat to be especially tender and tasty. January was a gloomy month. At first the sun barely peaked over the horizon. By the end of the month, there was light enough to see to read between 10:00 AM and 2:00 PM. Blizzards were commonplace the entire month, usually the coldest month in the Arctic with temperatures dropping as low as -50°F. On February 1 Crawford celebrated his 21st birthday.

There were a few more emotional incidents with Ada during the early part of 1922, but then the troubles ceased. Knight recorded: "February 9 and 25: The woman has been working diligently for a long time and excepting an occasional spell of crying seems to be contented . . . For the last few days the woman has been doing all the cooking, dishwashing, and scullery work besides sewing and mending and doing it very well."

Frequent snowstorms blew over their camp in early March, and Knight noted continuing temperatures of -40°F. Galle had his 20th birthday on March 6. Trapping was poor. Although they found an occasional fox in the traps, they had to share with the dogs some of the rolled oats and rice they had brought for themselves. Vic, the cat, did surprisingly well. She found things to eat and took great delight in teasing the dogs. At night, she crawled into one of the sleeping bags, seeming to have no preference who was with her as long as she could stay warm.

Knight shot a seal, but once again it drifted away before he could recover it. He described Galle and Crawford's extended bear hunt as they tried to keep up with the dogs

Allan Crawford with dogs while out hunting for seals and ducks.
Courtesy of Dartmouth College Library, Rauner Special Collections

chasing the bears. He concluded, "After six hours the hunters returned stating the bear had kept on going regardless of the dogs. They saw several fairly fresh bear tracks but the going was nearly impossible, for often they sank to their waists, and to their knees at nearly every step. Fed the last of the bear meat [to dogs], and unless another bear appears soon shall have to start cooking again." He showed no alarm about their situation but rather revealed the same confidence that Wrangel was such good game country that they didn't need to take the precautions that were necessary elsewhere.

As spring approached, flocks of ducks appeared from the south, and the honks of white geese, seagulls, and terns filled the air as the birds circled the camp. The snow began to vanish, and grass sprouted in some of the spongy areas. This was arctic spring. The sun never set, and seals abandoned their holes and came up on the ice to bask in the sun's warmth. The men resumed their attempts to capture a seal. However, catching them was not easy.

Actually, seal hunting was an art not usually mastered by white men. The seal is a suspicious animal, and while it dozes on the ice, it always positions itself on the edge of an open water channel or beside a breathing hole. In those days, that meant a hunter had to crawl toward the seal until he got within about 200 yards—where he stopped and lay on the ice, pretending to sleep.

The seal would go back to sleep for two or three minutes after it was convinced that it and the hunter were alike. That was all the time the hunter had to edge on his belly within 50 yards of the animal and take a shot. Sneaking up on a seal was difficult because at the first hint of danger, the seal plunged into the water. The four men stalked eight seals before they caught one. Throughout his diary, Knight showed no concern about their not catching any particular animal. He and the others apparently thought they could always catch the next one.

Despite spring's arrival, April was stormy and snowy. Most of the men stayed close to camp but Galle explored inland for a couple days. Knight recorded in his diary what Galle told him: "He camped the first night in the hills in a snowhouse after climbing a peak 1950 feet high. He was unable to see very far to the north because of a ridge farther on. He then went to the other camp, where he found the tent slightly damaged by a bear, which had made a hole in the roof of the storm shed. In two different places he found where a female bear had given birth to cubs. Saw a few bear and fox tracks, also several snow buntings."

May 10 brought Ada's 24th birthday. In the middle of the month, they pitched a new tent about 100 yards from the old one, which was tattered, torn, and soggy from the melting snow blocks. Along the shore they enjoyed temperatures in the low fifties; inland those temperatures rose to the low seventies. Filled with a renewed spirit, Knight wrote about Ada for the first time in several months: "May 27, 1922: I have not said anything much for a long time about the seamstress but will take the time now to say that she is doing as well as anyone could wish. Although we did not bring her along as a cook and dishwasher, she insists on doing that work as well as the sewing. She is still homesick sometimes."

With summer's arrival in June, the hunting improved as temperatures rose. Knight wrote, "At last!!! Crawford got a seal while out taking a few soundings [measures of the depth of water] through cracks and seal holes. A nice shot at 80 yards. A medium male, not very fat." During the rest of the summer season, the men caught over 40 seals. About this time the five started to look forward to seeing the relief ship that Stefansson had promised would bring food, ammunition, materials, and persons to replace the expedition members if they wanted to return to Nome.

The men talked and talked about whether they would stay or go home when the ship arrived. All of them were homesick for their families but they didn't want to disappoint Stefansson, who had trusted them to carry out the exploration and to claim the island for Great Britain. Ada, however, had had enough of Wrangel Island, and she definitely planned to return to Nome, despite the fact that

Knight noted in his diary on June 29: "I wish to state here that the seamstress is doing extremely well and is cheerful."

The favorable summer weather produced a profusion of wildflowers blooming on the tundra. Ada and Galle often walked among the blooms and grass and even took some of the flowers back to camp. Crawford and Maurer used the time to hunt seals, geese, and ducks, and Ada tried her hand at fishing as she had done in Alaska. She had no success though.

Tundra

Wrangel Island is covered with tundra, a vast, flat treeless area in which the subsoil is always frozen. The tundra changes its appearance drastically depending upon the season and the temperatures. In May the sun grows stronger, melting the snow quickly. As a result many lakes and rivers appear in the tundra. By the end of June, summer transforms the landscape. More than 400 varieties of wild plants grow on the island. Because the summer is so short, the flowers seem to explode as they quickly bloom. At that time, the tundra is topped with beautiful, colorful ground cover. When winter returns with its plunging, often below-freezing temperatures, nature seems to go to sleep, and the tundra loses its color as snow and ice cover the island.

Arctic cottongrass on tundra at Doubtful Harbour on Wrangel Island.
Morales/age fotostock

Knight took one of the dogs and explored the island. Between July 7 and July 12, he moved along the coast and visited two of the camps abandoned by *Karluk* survivors in 1914. For three days he and the dog endured heavy rains. The weather hindered him from catching much food—only a duck and two almost-meatless birds. When the rain ceased and he turned back toward camp, both he and the dog had painful feet and felt weak from lack of food.

On Knight's way back to the base camp, he came to the Skeleton River, a large stream on the island. In size it reminded him of the 11-mile-long Yamhill River in his native state of Oregon. When he had left camp to explore the island, he managed to cross the water on an ice bridge. But now the bridge had melted.

The mouth of the river was 250 feet wide, and the current was swift and strong. Hoping to find a shallow place to cross, he searched the banks without success for eight hours. His legs ached from plowing through the snow. Finally, he managed to find a shallower spot, and he and the dog plunged their way across the frigid waters. Once on the other side, he still had five miles to walk to camp. Half-dead at the time, he later recorded the experience in his diary:

> Occasionally I tried likely looking places for a crossing and, although I found places that I do not think were more than shoulder deep, the current was so rapid that to keep one's footing was impossible. Finally I decided to swim the river, so, putting my kodak, films, matches, etc., in a pair of water boots, across we went. I did not put my trusty watch in the water boots. It stopped then and I lost track of the time. After traveling about five hours more through snow, mud and water, I reached the camp site at Rodgers Harbour. Had a sleep and rest, then went to the old trapping camp, had another sleep, and reached home at 7 P.M. the evening of July 12th footsore and weary.

It was at this point that Knight's health gradually started deteriorating, a surprising development since he had endured much worse incidents in previous Arctic expeditions.

The men caught several seals in the next couple weeks despite the ice breaking up and moving around in pieces. In a letter he prepared to send to his parents when the relief ship arrived, Knight wrote:

> All along through July we got seals galore. Maurer and Galle being the sealers. Crawford spent a large part of his time traveling up in the mountains doing geological work and as I was the only one who knew how to make seal pokes [bags for storing and preserving food] and care for the skins, I stayed in camp and did that work. Up where I was before the making of pokes is the woman's job but this female of ours was brought up in a mission so she knows nothing of that work. We got altogether about 40 seals and have [saved in addition to what has been used from day to day] over a thousand pounds of blubber against next winter if the ship does not come.

August brought sunshine for several consecutive days. The earlier summer months had been mostly foggy and rainy with occasional sleet and snow. Galle had no scientific experiments like the other men, so he developed an interest in preparing food and enjoyed creating menus. Apparently at his suggestion, the group decided to try a different cooking method—frying. Up to that time, they had been following the Eskimo tradition of boiling food. Knight confirmed Galle's involvement in the food preparation by noting in his diary that their youngest member had put polar bear fat in cans and then used some of the fat to fry some bear steaks, which everyone enjoyed.

One of Galle's notes, dated August 14, showed that he didn't have much else to do:

> Bet with Knight that President of U.S. gets a salary of $75,000 a year plus traveling expenses of $25,000. $5. bet. Weather fair with variable winds. All stayed in camp to-day. The bear meat I boiled for breakfast and fried for myself and Ada did not taste like the previous bear meat. All had boiled meat, even K[night], & all agreed to taste. C boiled some bear blubber which tasted good. About 10:30 P.M. the largest flock of geese white flew west, extimated [sic] to have been upward to a thousand.

Food, weather conditions, and daily activities predominated in Galle's notes. He wrote about making a heart-shaped bookmark out of an ivory mastodon tusk he discovered on the beach. Other times he described the food: soup made with duck meat, roots, and the last of the barley they had brought with them. On August 15 he mentioned using the lantern for the first time, although they had burned candles for several prior days because of the heavy clouds. In brief notes intended only as reminders to himself for his longer journal, Galle described the group's activities on August 17:

> Weather still the same, all stay in. About 6 P.M. Ada spots bear offshore on ice ready to take to water. All

went on beach, K on big ice, I next about 100 yds. Further west, M 75 yds further in hole, C 500 yds further
at river. Bear swims to M, shot 3 times still in water.
I once launch dory. K. C. M. skin, female. All take pictures. I cut all possible blubber to try out, stop at 1:30
A.M. fill lard can & #2. Hear & see walrus while skinning bear . . . I have decided to stop eating hardbread
after this box. Put piece of bear liver in alcohol.

Because of its high vitamin A content, polar bear liver
was highly poisonous if eaten.

Galle mentioned Ada briefly but frequently in his notes,
showing that she had become an involved member of the
team. He described both his and Crawford's picture-taking
and their attempts to develop the film. Crawford was more
successful than Galle in this endeavor. The other few diary
entries from Galle showed no concern about a lack of food.
Even on good weather days, the men stayed around the
camp.

On August 25, Galle wrote, "Sun out all day, snow dis-
appears in short time. C prints pictures. All stay in. Tide
very high noon & midnight, current west flow, east ebb." A
month later on September 29, his comment is almost iden-
tical, "Weather good . . . all stay in; nothing attempted."
Surely if they had been concerned about a food shortage
they would have taken advantage of the good weather
to hunt game. Once again, their optimism led them to
inaction.

In September, night and day were almost equal in length.
The men observed the summer Arctic custom of sleeping

in the daytime and being awake at night, illogically carrying on a practice begun when there was perpetual sunlight. Again Galle's scribbled notes indicated this: "We go to bed at about 6 A.M., thick fog then. Get up 3 P.M., still thick, stayed [in camp] rest time, shortly before midnight fog lifted bit and could see to Mts. Ada scraped more seal skin. K wants her to scrape hair off skin, then that I cut lashing for him so he can repair sled." That day Ada made a stew of walrus heart and roots that appealed to the men.

Although there had been no mention of food shortages yet, Galle noted that he made "the suggestion to Crawford to break out one box hard bread and to issue each day two to each [person] . . . making ten a day, one box lasting about twenty days. Advised frying [them] in [bear] oil. Crawford approves and we start today." But the food situation was finally admitted near the end of the month. Knight's diary revealed they were running short on coffee, tea, sugar, beans, flour, and canned goods. About all that remained in any quantity of the food they had brought was pilot bread, a hard, flat, cracker made from flour, water, and sometimes salt.

Conditions for catching seals were bad because the ice was in constant motion and the ice floes that remained were covered with puddles of water. The four men again felt the lack of an umiak. Game had been plentiful that spring, but unfortunately, the men had not spent enough time capturing and storing meat in preparation for the time when everything was frozen, the seals went back into their holes, and the birds flew south. In his previous experiences Knight had often seen provisions dwindle to a few pounds only to be fully supplemented with the next day's catch. In other words, for him there was always another day to hunt. Apparently, the other men relied on his experience.

Meet Lorne Knight

Errol Lorne Knight's round, rosy cheeks, light brown hair, and blue eyes contrasted with his 230-pound, six foot tall body. Enthusiasm exuded from him, and his loud voice was frequently heard booming with laughter, making him seem 10 years younger. The son of John Irvine Knight, an insurance salesman, and his wife, Georgia Hoberg Knight, Lorne had been born in Hillsboro, Oregon, on June 6, 1893. Four years later the family moved to Washington, where Lorne attended public schools in Seattle and developed an interest in the lands to the north.

After just one year of high school, Lorne, who was developed beyond his years both physically and mentally, decided to quit school and go to work in a print shop. Later he did some land surveying. During that time his family moved to McMinnville, Oregon. Lorne was especially close to his mother, but it was his younger brother Joe who led Lorne to his first opportunity to explore the north.

Joe had found a scrawny cat abandoned on the road-side in a gunny sack. He named the cat Mike but did not take him home because of his mother's beloved pet canary. Then one day the cat disappeared. Joe and Lorne searched the neighborhood to no avail. A short time later, a knock sounded at their door. A man stood there holding Mike. Although his own children wanted to keep the cat, he had come to return it to Joe, who had been seen earlier playing with it.

Since Joe could not keep the animal at home, he let the man's two younger children keep it. The man invited Joe and Lorne to visit the cat any time they wanted, and a few days later the boys did. At that time Lorne learned that the man was a well-known whaler, Captain Louis L. Lane.

Captain Lane was planning to sail the *Polar Bear* to the Arctic, and he asked Lorne if he would like to go with him. Lorne eagerly accepted, and when the 55-ton whaler sailed on March 24, 1915, 22-year-old Lorne Knight was aboard the ship as a sailor. Some time later when the *Polar Bear* was anchored off Banks Island at Cape Kellett, Canada, the crew noticed a man trying to get their attention from the icy beach. Assuming it was an Eskimo seeking help, Captain Lane selected a small crew, including Lorne, and headed to the beach to see what the man wanted. To their surprise, they met a blond white man with a long, unkempt sandy beard.

He turned out to be the famous Arctic explorer Vilhjalmur Stefansson, who had been assumed dead for several years, ever since he departed the *Karluk*. An astonished

Whaling

Whalers are fishermen who hunt whales, although whales are mammals, not fish. The hunting of whales goes back thousands of years. The huge animals were prized for the products they provided. The oil from a whale's blubber was used for both lubricating precision machinery parts and for lighting. Once the whale was killed, usually by using a harpoon, the skin and blubber were peeled off in long strips that were then boiled to make whale oil. The whale bones provided material for candles and corsets.

The whaling industry prospered until the 1850s with whaling captains often displaying their wealth by building large houses in the best neighborhoods. With the invention of the oil well, the demand for whale oil plummeted, and the era of the great whaling ships ended. However, Herman Melville kept the public continually aware of the industry with his book *Moby-Dick*.

Captain Lane shouted to the other men, "Don't a dam [*sic*] one of you move till I shake hands with him!" After the two men met, Stefansson told Captain Lane that he was worried about a huge cargo of supplies he had on Herschel Island. He chartered the *Polar Bear* to take him to go get them. Lorne was excited to have time to listen to the great explorer's stories about where he had been and what he had been doing for the past several years.

After this meeting with Stefansson, Knight joined the Canadian expedition as part of the Northern Party and for four years studied the skills of surviving in the Arctic, although Knight's own survival seemed questionable at one point when he developed scurvy. He was saved by the appearance of a herd of caribou, which provided him the necessary fresh meat. Before the end of the expedition, Stefansson named Knight Harbour on northern Banks Island for Lorne Knight, placing him on the map. Lorne had kept a diary of his experiences, and it was later published by a family friend, Richard Montgomery, who called it *Pechuck: The Arctic Adventures of Lorne Knight*.

After their return from the Canadian expedition, Stefansson became a lecturer on the Circuit Chautauqua, and in 1921 Knight also joined the circuit to tell about his Arctic experiences and to help with the lantern slides during Stefansson's lectures. For a brief time, Knight served as a motorcycle policeman in Oregon. He was eager to leave that job behind and join the Wrangel Island expedition when he heard Stefansson talking about it. Stefansson was pleased to choose him as one of the expedition members, and Knight returned to McMinnville to say good-bye to his family and to his girlfriend, Doris Jones. Knight left for Seattle, where he would meet the other men chosen by Stefansson.

Lantern Slides

Lantern slides had their origin in the 17th century in devices called magic lanterns. The glass slides were originally hand painted using transparent oil paint, dyes made of a colorless, oily liquid, or watercolors. When dry, the slides were placed in the small wooden box called a magic lantern. Then, using an artificial light source and a combination of lenses, the small images were projected on a wall or screen.

In 1849, about 10 years after the invention of photography, photographs replaced the hand-painted images on slides used in the magic lanterns. They became popular for both entertainment and educational purposes, especially to accompany lectures, because they could allow large audiences to see the pictures.

As research progressed, mass-produced kits became available. Most of the mass-produced slides were in black and white. Hand coloring of the slides required skilled labor, space, and tools, and slowed down production. Because such coloring required the same artistic skills used by women who painted designs on china or other glass, they often provided the labor to colorize slides.

The use of lantern slides lasted until the 1950s when smaller transparencies became available along with the discovery of the Kodachrome process that made 35 mm slides less expensive to produce.

4

FADING HOPES

ALTHOUGH THERE WERE TIMES when the men had plenty of fresh meat, consistently getting enough was difficult. They were once able to capture a couple of walruses that came close enough to shore for them to seize the huge animals. These in addition to some birds, foxes, and an occasional polar bear kept them going until mid-summer. They had little success with the few seals that stayed long distances from shore, and the surf was too turbulent to use the 700-pound dory to go after them.

Catching more walruses would have solved their food problems. Ironically, they could hear a great many of the huge black-skinned creatures offshore but they were too far away to be seen and too far to go after because of the ice. However, nothing in Knight's diary indicated an awareness of how bad off they could be if they didn't catch another

Men in the dory, trying to move through the water to catch seals or walruses. *Courtesy of Dartmouth College Library, Rauner Special Collections*

walrus. Since they didn't have an umiak or a walrus harpoon, they didn't even try to capture one of the distant animals.

Then late one day, using their binoculars, they saw a herd of about 20 of the one-ton walruses on an ice floe to the southwest approximately two miles away. The water was covered with young ice and large floes, so the men decided it would be safer to wait until daylight to go after the animals. By the next morning the walruses had disappeared, although the men could hear them off and on throughout the day.

Two walruses finally came nearer. From their tent they could see two of the huge animals lying by themselves on a small cake of ice southeast of the camp, away from the bigger pack of animals. Excited, the men dragged the dory across the beach, down to the water, and launched it. This was the opportunity they had waited for—walrus on the ice. All four went to hunt them.

Three of the men made a landing on a nearby cake of ice about 150 yards from their intended prey. Knight stayed in the boat while the others crept across the ice, keeping out of sight behind a pressure ridge—a ridge that occurs when great sheets of ice collide. At the point of collision, these ridges of ice build up, often reaching 5 to 10 feet or more above adjacent stretches of level ice. From this hiding place, all three men fired at the same time. Maurer's and Galle's bullets hit their mark, but Crawford's went astray. The men got back in the dory and rowed over to examine their catch. The dead were a large female and her half-grown calf. The hunters were in high spirits!

But they had a problem. Darkness was approaching, and they didn't want to leave their catch and risk losing it on a shifting ice pack. Galle got in the dory and rowed back to camp to get an ax and a lantern so that they could see to cut the animal into more manageable pieces. The others stayed behind on the ice to skin the animals. They had just finished skinning the cow when Galle returned. While he was gone, moving ice had blocked his path and separated the others from him and the boat. The three were floating helplessly on an ice floe. Their only means of escape was to get in the dory several hundred yards away.

Small, swiftly moving pieces of ice between them and the boat stuck up like rocks in a river but were not stable. Realizing that Galle by himself could not bring the dory to them, Crawford dashed across the ice field. The shifting ice cakes occasionally came together so that he could step on them but then separated leaving channels of water between them. With the help of a pole, Crawford jumped from ice cake to ice cake and reached the dory. He and Galle then tried to reach Knight and Maurer but failed again and again to move the heavy boat toward the other two men.

The dory was so heavy and the ice so thick that steering the boat was impossible. Taking as much meat as they could carry, Maurer and Knight tried to replicate Crawford's jumps across the ice cakes to reach the dory. By that time, it was after midnight and the ice was moving so swiftly that their many attempts were unsuccessful. Finally, the ice stood still long enough for them to reach the dory by holding on to ropes attached to it.

By lantern light, the four tried to move the dory through the water and then drag it over the ice to the walrus meat. But the ice was too rough and the boat too heavy. They had to leave their meat catch behind and go back to camp at about 2:00 AM. During the rest of the day, the ice stilled and about 4:00 PM they launched the dory again to go retrieve some of the meat. They could not get the boat any closer than a quarter mile and went back for a sled to go the rest of the way across the ice.

After hauling the sled over insecure ice cakes, they arrived at the meat, which by then had provided meals for ravens and gulls. Tracks showed that a polar bear had walked by during the night but luckily for them had ignored the meat. They loaded the sled with about 600 pounds of blubber and walrus skin and started back to the dory.

They had almost reached the boat when a channel of water opened across their path. They could not carry the meat and skin across open water, so they had to unload the sled. They divided the catch and loaded half of it back on the sled. However, they failed to tie the load down; the sled tipped on its side, and everything slid into the sea. By the end of the day they had salvaged only 50 pounds of meat—a shoulder and a liver—barely enough to feed them and the dogs for one day. That night they fried the tough but palatable walrus meat. Before many days had passed, Knight stated in his diary that they were out of meat again.

Only a brief time existed during the summer months for a ship to get through the ice-choked Chukchi Sea. The five watched and waited, although Knight expressed no concern in his diary about the ship not having arrived. Ada, however, spent much of her time on the hillsides looking across the frozen Chukchi Sea for signs of open water.

Back in Canada, Stefansson was begging the government for money to send a relief ship. The Canadian government provided no assistance but instead referred him to London to meet with the minister of the colonies. The British government was not immediately responsive. They wanted to discuss the sovereignty of Wrangel Island with several other nations before committing monetary support. Stefansson's good friend Orville Wright gave him $3,000 (equivalent to about $42,000 in today's currency), and after Stefansson made another humanitarian plea to the Canadian government, he received another $3,000.

Orville Wright

Orville Wright, along with his brother Wilbur, made aviation history when they designed, built, and flew the world's first airplane. Born in 1871 in Dayton, Ohio, Orville enjoyed a childhood that allowed him the freedom to pursue his interests. His love of bicycle riding led to his first business, a bicycle repair and sales shop, where he experimented with and applied his mechanical talents.

The brothers started researching aerodynamics after they saw similarities between cycling and flying. Their drive and talent led to the invention of the airplane and the first manned flight at Kitty Hawk, North Carolina, on December 17, 1903. After Wilbur died in 1912, Orville, who never married, pursued other interests. He spent the last three decades of his life serving on boards and committees related to aeronautics, including the National Advisory Committee for Aeronautics, the predecessor to the National Aeronautics and Space Administration (NASA). On January 30, 1948, at the age of 76, Orville died after suffering a second heart attack. He is buried at the Wright family plot in Dayton, Ohio.

During all the time that Stefansson was seeking financial backing, the relatives of the four men on the island
bombarded him with requests for information about the
relief ship—when it would go to Wrangel, how they could
send letters and packages. But Stefansson did not get the
financial backing in time for the *Teddy Bear*, with Captain
Joe Bernard at the helm, to get through the frigid waters
around Wrangel before they became a solid mass of ice.

The schooner departed Nome on August 20, 1922, at 4:00
PM, carrying Bernard, three other white men, and some
Eskimos who could replace any of the original party who
wanted to go home. Even though the trip was hazardous,
the ship was expected back in two weeks. On the morning
after their departure, they ran into a heavy northwestern
wind, causing them to pull into shelter at Cape York.

On that same day on Wrangel, Galle noted on a scrap of
paper that they saw 14 bears, 5 of which were cubs. However, he made no mention of killing any of them for food.
The men might have made more of an effort to catch and
freeze meat if they had known about the troubles the *Teddy
Bear* was encountering—the worst ice conditions in the last
25 years.

For several days the *Teddy Bear* crew endured gale force
winds that kept them anchored, unable to move toward
the island. Not until August 28 were they able to start push-
ing their way through the ice. They made a little progress
but then were stopped for another two days. On Wrangel,
a note later found among Galle's papers confirmed that ice
farther out was solid: "I go for short walk . . . I could see ice
from high places on tundra pretty sparsely strewn about

two miles offshore; from there on an almost solid mass as far as I could see, about eight or ten miles."

The ship was still 100 miles from Wrangel Island in early September, waiting at the outskirts of a solidly frozen ice pack to get through. After receiving word from another schooner, the *Sea Wolf*, that it had been forced to turn back, Bernard decided there was no point in trying to go farther on the route he had chosen. He decided to try another way. But turning around was difficult because of the ice around them. They had to pull the ship with a system of

Teddy Bear stuck in ice on its way to Wrangel Island with replacement supplies. *Courtesy of Dartmouth College Library, Rauner Special Collections*

ropes and pulleys as they cut their way back through the ice. This helped only temporarily, and the ship was soon trapped again. The only hope was to reach an open channel of water.

Bernard found such a channel late one night but decided to wait until daylight to proceed. On the morning of September 5, just at daylight, he entered what the night before had been open water. Now it was covered with ice about one-inch thick. However, the ship made some progress for the rest of the day. Then the winds came back, and the ice again closed in on the *Teddy Bear*. Penetrating the ice wall seemed impossible, and Bernard was running out of supplies for his crew. Finally, after several attempts, he turned the ship back toward Nome, which they reached on September 22.

In a later, day-by-day report to Stefansson, Bernard explained the circumstances that caused him to turn back: "We had to press the vessel quite hard to break the ice in many places. The vessel suffered some damage by being stove in and also the propeller was bent, both blades hitting the ice, so that it was practically disabled." Unfortunately for the Wrangel expedition, the ice did not break up until late fall of that year.

Stefansson was not particularly concerned when he didn't get messages from the men. He expected that in the winter they would walk to the nearest wireless radio station in either Russia's Emma Harbor or Nome. From there they could send him a wireless message. Surprisingly, he did not consider such a journey of over 100 miles long or difficult. He wrote assurances about their well-being in a letter to Galle's father: "They are just as safe on their island as Robinson Crusoe was on his—a little more so because there are no cannibals in that vicinity." Whether he thought about Ada's situation at all is not known.

Rain poured on Wrangel, leaving behind a fresh breeze from the east. But as far as the five expedition members could see, the ice was not moving, although there appeared to be water a long way off. By the end of September, a year after their landing on Wrangel, they had about given up hope of seeing a relief ship that year. Among Galle's notes were constant comments about their sleep patterns as the nights became as long as the days. He also mentioned that others besides Knight were not feeling well and were perhaps showing early signs of scurvy: "C seemed very tired & worn, dragged his feet . . . M continually complaining about his back, wrenched some weeks ago; and all complaining about being exceptionally sleepy today."

Their hope for a relief ship surged for a short time when a strong gale from the west moved across the island and set the ice in rapid motion. About a mile offshore a wide channel of water appeared, running east and west. To the south they saw a great expanse of water sky, the dark appearance of a cloud layer when it is over a surface of open water. This was an indication the ice was breaking up.

Knight wrote in his diary on October 4: "The water sky noted yesterday is still visible, and I am sure that the whole ocean is open outside this belt of ice that is hanging to the beach." He was right. For a while they hung a lantern from the flag pole and kept it lighted in case a ship passed them in the darkness. By mid-October the rough surf had pounded

Scurvy

Scurvy is a nutritional deficiency caused by insufficient amounts of vitamin C. Symptoms of the disease usually begin about three months after not getting enough of the vitamin. They include fatigue, irritability, pain in the legs, and the appearance of small red-blue spots on the skin.

If not treated, other symptoms develop, including swollen gums that bleed or soften to the point that teeth loosen or fall out. Joints may bleed, causing severe pain. Shortness of breath is common after physical activity. Another characteristic of scurvy is that it breaks down capillaries and the least amount of pressure causes them to rupture and bleed. Untreated, scurvy also causes jaundice, a yellowing of the skin and eyes from liver failure, and edema, swelling caused by the buildup of fluids in the body. Fatal heart problems may also develop.

Humans must get vitamin C from outside the body; it is not something that the body produces for itself. The best sources are fruits, vegetables, and foods fortified with the vitamin. Meat contains very small amounts of the vitamin. Since fresh fruits and vegetables are not available in the Arctic, explorers have long eaten almost raw animal meat to prevent scurvy. Vitamin C easily loses its effectiveness when exposed to heat and water. The connection between scurvy and vitamin C was not made until 1932.

the belt of ice near the beach to pieces, and the whole area immediately around Wrangel Island was clear of ice. Big waves rolled in over the beach.

The welcome appearance of a female polar bear and her two cubs toward the end of the month was chronicled in Knight's diary: "Everything comes to him who waits, or goes after it. At 7 A.M. the dogs set up a howl. Crawford rushed out, and about 100 feet west of the tents stood a female bear and two cubs. He killed them in seven shots. The cubs proved to be yearlings." There was very little blubber on any of the bears, but everyone, including the dogs, ate until they were full. Each animal kill added to Ada's store of furs to make into clothing.

With winter's arrival, the blue surface of the sea around Wrangel turned white as it froze over. A large expanse of floating ice came in from the north. No one bothered to fill the beacon lantern swinging from the flag pole. There was no use. No ship could reach them now. They would have to spend a second winter on the island. The first winter had been an adventure with hardships they could handle. They would have quickly forgotten those bad times if the relief ship had come as expected. Instead they now began to store as much meat as they could catch and rationed their other meager resources. They had only about two months' worth of dog feed left and had also exhausted the supply of wood for about two miles on either side of the camp.

They moved the camp to Doubtful Harbour on November 15, 1922. There they had a plentiful supply of wood for fuel, thus conserving their animal fat, but they needed a polar bear to come along so they could feed the hungry dogs. The day before the move, Knight wrote: "For a long time I have said nothing about our seamstress. She is very quiet and rather downhearted over the fact that the ship did not show up, but she keeps busy and is at present making a pair of fancy moose-hide mittens. There is considerable clothing to be made for Crawford and me if we go to Siberia, but I will not have her start until we get moved." At that time his and Crawford's plans to make the trek depended on ice conditions, available dog food for the five dogs, and the weather.

The plans had not been shared with Galle, probably because he had no experience to contribute to the decision-making. Maurer and Knight had both been on previous Arctic expeditions, and Crawford was head of the team because of his Canadian citizenship. However, Galle had overheard snatches of conversation that indicated they planned to go somewhere. With the move to the second camp, Knight revealed to Galle that he and Crawford planned to walk to Nome. In his journal, Galle commented:

On way back K tells me that they, C & K were probably going to Nome next spring, does not say why. Tells me will need lots of money, asks if I have any. Will loan all ($2.50). K keeps conversation pretty nonsensical. Of course, I could ask questions but not up to me. I can figure their motives. Will note now they will not go to Nome or even Siberia. We shall await developments. Was informed (K) he would not like to go but had to.

Nothing in Galle's notes indicated where or whether he thought they might go.

The little food supply continued to dwindle as winter stretched on, and fresh meat became a luxury. They did not have enough food to last until spring, even though their daily fare had been reduced to hard bread and seal oil. By that time they were feeding bearskin and blubber to the dogs. The lack of proper food for the explorers and Ada was affecting their health, especially that of Knight, who was starting to show signs of scurvy.

Knight noted on December 12: "The woman is doing wonderful work and is a great deal better than a year ago." By then she had almost completed clothing outfits for Knight and Crawford for their proposed journey to seek help. Just before their second Christmas on the island, the snow hardened enough that blocks could be cut to put a roof on the tents at their new site. Knight felt ill and could not help with the work. Although he claimed the symptoms were indigestion, they were the onset of the disease that would eventually ravage his strong body.

Christmas came, but the five people barely observed it. They had no potatoes, no coffee, and no tobacco. Hard bread, walrus skin, and seal oil made up their Christmas dinner. They had celebrated the previous evening by each having one extra piece of hard bread. With the snow roof completed that day, they were at least warm and comfortable on Christmas Eve. On Christmas Day Knight finished a new dog harness for the trip, while Crawford made a ridge pole and uprights for the tent they would use if they found themselves in a place where there was not enough

Milton Galle scraping animal skin to soften it to be made into clothing.
Courtesy of Dartmouth College Library, Rauner Special Collections

snow to build a snow house. The two continued preparations by repairing the sled while the other men went out to check the traps, hoping desperately to find a catch.

Meet Allan Crawford

Twenty-year-old Allan Crawford saw an opportunity for some excitement. He had just completed the third year of his studies at the University of Toronto when one of his professors showed him a letter from Arctic explorer Vilhjalmur Stefansson seeking young men trained in botany, zoology, or geology to participate in a privately funded polar expedition.

Displaying an avid curiosity and eagerness for new experiences, Allan was attracted to the project. Oldest of the three children of University of Toronto professor John Thomas Crawford and his wife, Helen, Allan was close to his family but had led an uneventful life. He immediately replied to the letter and assured Stefansson that he met the physical requirements specified in the communication—5 foot 10 in height, weight 151 pounds, above-average vision without glasses, a strong heart with good circulation, no serious contagious diseases, a good walker, and no tendency toward numbness in hands or feet.

Crawford had won honors in his math and science studies and had served in the Officers' Training Corps in Canada. He had been underage for an overseas assignment, so he sought a different activity and helped to found *The Goblin*, the university's humorous magazine for which he served as circulation manager.

Crawford's response impressed Stefansson, and he invited the young man to meet him at Ann Arbor, Michigan, where Stefansson was lecturing. The June 29, 1921, meeting was mutually successful, but Stefansson could not make a firm offer until he was sure he had acquired funding for the expedition.

In July Stefansson's business partner, Alfred J. T. Taylor, contacted Crawford and offered him a contract for the Wrangel Island expedition at a salary of $1,800 per year. Allan accepted it and said a quick good-bye to his family before heading to Seattle, Washington, to meet the other three members of the team and to join them and Stefansson on the Circuit Chautauqua. Upon arrival, he learned that, although he had no Arctic experience, Stefansson had named him leader of the team because of his Canadian/British citizenship. However, he was cautioned that Lorne Knight and Fred Maurer, due to their experience, must participate in all major decisions.

INSTRUCTIONS TO CRAWFORD

Always remember the following: Although I [Stefansson] have confidence in you, you are in command through the accident of being British while Knight

The Goblin

The University of Toronto's humorous undergraduate magazine, *The Goblin*, began in 1921 and was published seven times a year from November to May. An annual subscription cost $1.25. The editorial policy was to make readers laugh.

Stephen Leacock, who became the world's best-known humorist in the English-speaking world during the early 20th century, was a contributor. In his "Sermon on Humour," he set the standard by quoting Charles II, "Good jests ought to be like lambs, not dogs; they should cut, not wound." The magazine carried humorous contributions from other students and "borrowed" stories and jokes from other similar publications.

By today's standards, the typical jokes were silly:

He: Lunch with me?
She: Yes, where'll we go?
He: Let's eat up the street.
She: No thanks; I don't care for asphalt.

And

Grace: I told him he mustn't see me any more.
Brother: Well, what did he do?
Grace: He turned out the light.

and Maurer are not. They have valuable experience which you lack. The wiser you are the more you will follow the advice of your experienced men. If you can not reach the island in question you should spend the winter on the mainland . . . and cross over by sled in March or early April to raise the flag. This should be done no matter if men of our or any other nation are already on the island . . . whatever happens send me a night letter the first day after landing in Nome. You may give out any news that does not reveal anything confidential.

Crawford followed the instructions but never got a chance to communicate that to his sponsor.

5

TREACHEROUS TREKS

IN JANUARY THE SUN WAS so far below the horizon, even at noon on a cloudy day, that it was almost impossible for a person to see a polar bear until the two met face-to-face. It was the deadliest month, with darkness covering the island about 20 hours of each day. It was very dangerous to travel when there was so little sun and when storms frequently covered thin ice with a treacherous blanket of snow. Despite these conditions, as the new year began, Knight's diary entries showed an increased urgency about his and Crawford's proposed trip.

Why the men couldn't wait a few more weeks is not clear. But food for both the people and the dogs was an issue. So despite the winter's darkness and the dangers, Crawford and Knight decided to cross the frozen Chukchi Sea to Siberia, a distance of about 100 miles, and then travel on to Nome to get help. They planned to reach Nome in 60

Allan Crawford, titular head
of expedition, just before he
and Lorne Knight set out for
Siberia.
*Courtesy of Dartmouth College Library,
Rauner Special Collections*

or 70 days. Maurer, Galle, and Ada stayed behind. Knight and Crawford hoped to see the expedition's sponsor, Vilhjalmur Stefansson, at the end of their journey, but before they left, each man wrote a letter to him. He had told them prior to their leaving Nome that he was negotiating with the Canadian government to lead another expedition to explore territory north of Wrangel Island. Just in case he might have already started such a mission and they missed getting to see him, they wanted to tell him what had happened so far on Wrangel.

Adding to their need to write letters to Stefansson before they left was the realization of the dangers involved in what they planned. In his letter Crawford spoke of the scarcity of food and of his belief that fox trapping for furs would not be a profitable business, an idea Stefansson had asked him to research. Crawford also mentioned that he had taken his diary with him but that his scientific reports about his trips to the interior to explore the mountains were in his trunk at the camp. He had collected meteorological data, made a chart of the coastline, and had taken ocean soundings. All of this information he left behind. Knight's letter was brief and melancholy.

Although the weather had been cloudy and warm during most of December, a howling gale blew in with the onset of the new year. About six inches of soft snow covered the ground, and the two men decided to wait for it to pack. Crawford and Knight loaded their sled with meager supplies for 30 days—hard tack and seal blubber for themselves; a little dried meat and four sealskins for the dogs when the meat ran out. Their total load weighed about 700 pounds. They calculated they could reach Siberia in 30 days, where they could get food for themselves and their dogs before heading on to Nome. They fastened the five remaining dogs into the new harness that Knight had made and set out on January 7 at 1:00 AM.

They traveled due south and made good time for the first hour before encountering broken up young ice with soft snow in between. For two and a half hours, they traveled about a mile offshore along the edge of the rough ice closest to land. It was much rougher than ice farther out to sea because onshore winds or currents set the ice floes in motion, forcing them against land or ice attached to land. When the floes' edges met, they broke up and piled into rough ridges. Adding to Crawford's and Knight's problems was the increased darkness that caused the sled to tip over numerous times as they encountered mounds of snow. They finally stopped and made camp. They had traveled only about six miles east of Doubtful Harbour.

Lorne Knight with two of the dogs he and Crawford took with them in their attempt to reach Siberia.
Courtesy of Dartmouth College Library, Rauner Special Collections

By their second day of travel, the ice became as hard as concrete with little snow covering it. Walking was much easier, and Knight noted in his diary that except for pains in his legs at night, he was all right. After breaking camp about 9:30 on the third morning, they continued due south.

A short way from the beach, they unexpectedly encountered soft snow, and Knight had to get into the harness with the dogs to help pull the heavy load. About two miles offshore, they again encountered rough ice, which the dogs and the sled could not handle. The dogs were weak because they had not been getting the proper food. Hard bread and seal oil worked for a few days but did not keep up the animals' strength for long. Already the men were thinking about turning back.

Knight spelled out the grim situation in his diary:

> Crawford and I have been racking our brains on the best thing to do. Matters stand thus: We have only five dogs, a weak sled and not a great deal of provisions. The ice is so bad that we can not travel to sea or to open water, where we might obtain seals. I am nearly all in. (I hate to admit this, but I am sure I can not help it.) My scurvy has been coming back for the last month. When we started I was in hopes of getting fairly good going and a chance to get fresh meat, but my legs go back on me in this rough ice, for I'm forced to get in the harness to help the dogs.

Crawford and Knight huddled in their makeshift shelter of canvas and snow blocks on the ice off Cape Hawaii on the far southeastern part of the island. They had varying degrees of frostbite. Crawford's big toe on his right foot was frozen while Knight had deep cracks in both heels. Walking was difficult for both of them. At night Knight suffered from pain in his legs, and he developed hard, red

Fred Maurer, oldest member of team, in typical winter garb that he wore to go fox hunting.
Courtesy of Dartmouth College Library, Rauner Special Collections

pinpricks on his lower legs and arms. As it became evident that Knight's scurvy was affecting him more and more and making him weaker and weaker, he and Crawford conceded defeat. They reluctantly abandoned their hope of leaving Wrangel Island and decided to return to their companions at the main camp. Even that became a struggle as they faced strong gales and snow.

The three people who had been left behind at the camp tried to stay busy so that they would not think about the lack of food or the danger which their companions faced. Ada sewed and the men checked the traps. Maurer finally caught a fox—good news for their next meal.

In the evenings they told one another stories. Galle especially liked Ada's story called The Lady in the Moon.

Crawford and Knight, exhausted, stumbled back into camp on January 20 and saw the sun for the first time

Summary of The Lady in the Moon

An Eskimo girl ignored her parents' demands to marry. One day, she found a man's skull and hid it in the reindeer skins on her bed. Her father found the skull and thought it was the reason she wouldn't marry. He drove a sharp stone through one of its eyes and then flung the skull into the ocean. When the girl discovered the skull's fate, she threw herself into the ocean.

The fishes told her that the skull, now attached to a man, was on a nearby beach. When she found the skull man, he agreed to help her get back home if she did exactly what he told her. He showed her a path and warned her to take the left fork. She ignored his warning because the right trail was smoother.

After traveling a while, she came to the moon, where the man in the moon took her prisoner. A medicine man freed her and sent her to an old woman for protection. For many years, she lived with the old woman. But the girl missed her parents. Finally, the old woman told her how to get back to earth but warned that her landing was critical. If she landed with legs straight, she would be young. If she landed with legs bent, she would be old and stooped. Unable to keep her legs straight when she landed, she became an old woman. She slowly traveled to her parents' house but found only a sunken hole where it had once been.

since the midwinter twilight. Maurer, Galle, and Ada were shocked to see the men return because they thought by now the two must be nearing Siberia. Upon their return, the two travelers learned that the food situation was even more dire than when they left. They decided to go for help again.

This time all the men except Knight would make the trip. They believed three would fare better than two because they could divide the outside chores at the end of each day and get to shelter more quickly. Besides, there was not enough food at the camp to feed three people. Because of his developing scurvy, Knight stayed on Wrangel with Ada. How she felt about being left alone with the man who once scared her is not known. If she had fears, she kept them to herself and worked busily to make the clothing the men needed for their trip.

One of Maurer's letters, found after his death, began with a description of their food situation, "The chief reason for our leaving is the shortage of food. There is not adequate food for all, there being only ten twenty-pound pokes of seal oil to last until next summer." He also mentioned that he had discovered only a few minerals and no fossils. Later parts of the letter left the impression that he did not want to leave the island but agreed to go only to show respect for the party's leadership. Based upon what Maurer said in other letters to his family, his elder brother John later confirmed that Fred joined the trek to lend his experience of traveling on ice and to leave more food for Ada and Knight than if he had stayed behind.

A notation in Galle's scattered papers stated that he could not figure out why they would leave the island.

On the other hand, Crawford's January 7 letter indicated agreement with the decision: "When I saw how sparse seal and bear were I decided it would be unwise to stay here with the dogs all winter." Despite their diverse opinions, the men must not have argued much as plans proceeded rapidly. Knight wondered what people might say about his being alone with Ada, but he saw no other option. He showed his rationale for going ahead with the plan in a diary entry:

> I will remain here as camp keeper for the reason that I think I would be unwise to attempt the said trip . . . I am sure that anyone looking at this case clearly will see that there is nothing else to be done. It is impossible I think for two men to make the trip, I think, with only five dogs and as grub is short here, it is essential for this party to split . . . The woman and I will have about six hard bread each a day until the seals and birds arrive. This is not counting what foxes I hope to catch on the two trap lines that I intend to take over, or perhaps a bear. We will also have about five hundred pounds of seal fat and five or six gallons of bear oil.

The three worked hard to load their sled with supplies: hard bread and seal blubber, tents and tools. Crawford took with him his geological specimens, and all three carried their diaries. They fastened the five remaining dogs to their heavily loaded sled and set out on January 28, 1923, at 9:00 AM—a clear day that was bitterly cold, with temperatures hovering around -50°F. Circumstances for such a trek were less than ideal. Days were still short and dark, and the dogs were weak from the shortage of food.

But the three were optimistic and promised to return with a ship to get Ada and Knight. Then the little party headed due south and were soon out of sight. Inside her tent, Ada cried as the men left.

They were never heard from again. Ada later said: "I don't know what happened to them. Maybe they fell through the ice, or they could have been killed by a polar bear or Russians. I don't know."

Meet Frederick Maurer

Twenty-one-year-old Frederick Maurer was a fireman on the *Karluk* when it sank. He was one of the survivors who had spent six months in 1914 on Wrangel Island with scant supplies and food. Surprisingly, rather than make him want nothing more to do with Arctic exploration, Maurer's experiences made him eager to return to the challenges of the desolate island.

The son of David and Mary Maurer of New Philadelphia, Ohio, Frederick had one brother, John. Maurer became his hometown's hero when he returned from his adventures. His kind nature had led him to rescue the ship's cat, Niger-aurak, or "little black one" in the Inuit tongue, before the *Karluk* sank. He called the cat Nicki and managed to keep her alive throughout the bleak months on Wrangel Island. To keep the cat protected from the icy cold, he had made her a little deerskin bag in which to travel. He tied the bag's drawstrings around his neck, allowing the cat to snuggle to his chest for warmth.

After returning home, Maurer joined a Chautauqua lecture circuit, although one that visited smaller towns than the ones to which Stefansson and Knight went. When he

Ship's Fireman

A ship's fireman is responsible for keeping the fires burning in the ship's boilers that make steam and power for the large turbines that produce the ship's electricity and turn its propellers. Because of the heat, firemen often work stripped naked to the waist while perspiration rolls down their faces leaving tracks in the coal dust that covers them.

A fireman's first job is to use his shovel and an iron bar to break up large lumps of coal into fragments about the size of a man's fist. The next task must be coordinated with the roll and pitch of the ship so that the fireman does not lose his balance. He opens the door to a firebox and quickly uses his iron bar to clear the grates of previous ashes and cinders. This allows for a better draft of air across the burning coals. Then he shovels in a layer of coal, usually no more than four shovelfuls at one time. The fireman closes the firebox's door, being careful to avoid a draft that can send flames into his face. Firemen work in tandem with other crew members to maximize the amount of steam produced.

showed an interest in the Wrangel expedition, Stefansson got him a job as his second assistant so that he and Knight could become acquainted. The two men listened attentively to Stefansson's presentations and contributed their own experiences before or after their mentor's lectures. Despite the fact that Maurer was of a quieter, more thoughtful nature than the active Knight, the two seldom disagreed.

Maurer had a girlfriend, Delphine Jones of Miles, Ohio. They had not known each other very long, having met on the Chautauqua circuit. Her beauty and her stylish

Inuit Language

The name Inuit means "the people." Their language is called Inuktitut. However, there is a wide range of dialects throughout the large areas occupied by the Inuits. Inuits write in syllabics. For example, the symbol ^ represents "pi," while ˃ stands for "pu."

Many of the Inuktitut words are long and difficult for nonnatives to pronounce. For example, in order to wish good-bye to a single person, the Inuit says *tavvauvutit*, pronounced TAH-vow-voo-teet. If he needs a sled, he must request a *qamutik*, pronounced CAW-moo-tick. The variations among Inuits living in different locations make the language even more difficult for outsiders to understand.

wardrobe attracted Maurer. When she heard that he would be leaving on another expedition, she insisted they get married before he left and threatened suicide if they didn't. Unsure how to handle his emotional girlfriend and anxious to join the other men going to Wrangel, he agreed.

Because of the haste of their wedding, they had to quickly find a place to hold the ceremony. Stefansson, who had agreed to stand up as Maurer's best man, had some good friends in Missoula, Montana, who offered their house, which was near the site where Stefansson was lecturing. Delphine rode a train to Missoula, and she and Maurer married on August 11, 1921. Their honeymoon trip by train covered the 1,000 miles west to Seattle, Washington, where Maurer was to meet the rest of his expedition team. After Maurer departed for Nome, Delphine, now Mrs. Maurer, took the train back to Ohio. And the long wait began.

6

OH FOR A BEAR!

WITH THE THREE OTHER members of the team gone, Ada found herself alone with Lorne Knight, the man she had been so frightened of when they first arrived on Wrangel Island. But circumstances now dictated that the remaining two support each other.

Knight and Ada quickly realized that it made no sense for them to heat two separate living areas. To do so would require the gathering of more fuel. Instead Knight spent time fixing up the small shelter to be convenient for the two of them and placed a cot for Ada on the opposite side from his. The day after Crawford, Maurer, and Galle left, a strong gale from the east forced Knight and Ada to stay inside, where a wood-burning stove kept them warm and comfortable. Their shelter would be adequate until the snow started to melt in the spring. At that time the snow would have to be removed from all the outside boxes, and the walls and roof would have to be dug away.

Ada didn't realize at first how sick Knight was. One day he tried to walk a short distance to cut some wood but never made it because he fainted. When he didn't come back, Ada went to look for him and found him sprawled on the ground. He was unconscious for only a few seconds, and Ada breathed a sigh of relief.

By the time she got him back to his sleeping bag, he had developed a fever. Knight noted: "The woman is a great deal more frightened over my condition than I am. I don't deny that it is a rather mean position in which she finds herself, but she is wonderfully cheerful, and is now busy sharpening the wood saws. She insists on doing practically everything, and I willingly permit it." Thus began Ada's role as nurse and food provider.

Knight felt good only when sitting up or lying down. Hoping to prove to himself that he didn't really have scurvy, he scanned the encyclopedias they had brought with them, seeking more information about the symptoms of the disease. As he compared his situation to the symptoms, he found that he had about half of them to some degree. The others had not manifested themselves. Even so he was too weak to help with the chores.

For a short time Ada despaired, but one by one she assumed the tasks that Knight could no longer do—chopping wood, cutting ice to melt for water, visiting the traps, and resetting them. Her mission school training had not prepared her for a life in the vast, icy domain, but she learned how to deal with the elements in order to find food.

She became determined not to let the relentless forces of nature destroy her and her companion. She reminded herself: "Ada, Mr. Knight is sick now just like a little baby and I will take care of him just like my own little babies that are sick and die."

Knight's constant prayer was for a bear to appear. The only cure for scurvy was vitamin C, found in fresh raw meat, vegetables, and fruit. Since there was no way of securing the latter two, Knight needed fresh meat. He knew that in a few months the females would come out of their holes with their cubs, and then there would be plenty of meat. In the meantime Knight suffered from a painful left leg swollen just above the knee. Moving was difficult, but he knew the pain would go away if he could only get some fresh meat. He wrote: "I can see that I cannot go far away from camp and unless a bear walks into camp, I see small chance of getting one, for the woman cannot be trusted with my rifle. She is easily excited and knows nothing about a gun and this is the only rifle that . . . we have . . . Come on bear!"

An entry two weeks later showed Knight's worsening condition: "I feel as though I would like to get up but when I make a try I am dizzy as can be. I am as hungry as a wolf but it is all I can do to force down a few mouthfuls. If anyone hankered for anything I hanker for fresh raw meat and lots of it." Late in January a ferocious wind blew in from the east. Snow piled up against the outside door, and neither Knight nor Ada could get out. Although they and Vic, the cat, spent a cozy day protected from the elements, they worried about where their three companions might be and how they were faring in the strong windblown snow. February 1 was Crawford's 22nd birthday.

Before the men left, Maurer had given Knight his trap line map that covered about three miles. Ada took it and followed it to locate the traps. Then she taught herself how to set them and to cover them with snow so the foxes couldn't see them. This required a special skill on Wrangel because of the way the winds blew the snow. Covering the traps worked best when soft snow covered the trap just enough that the fox could not see it. However, the winds on Wrangel blew the snow into mounds that allowed the soft-footed foxes to move across them without tripping the trap's spring.

After Ada mastered the technique to set them, she checked every day for catches but with no luck. She later said: "When I was out I was afraid of meeting a polar bear, and every little while I would turn and look around to see if one was in sight, and if there had been one I would have fainted, for I only had a snow knife with me and I didn't know what to do to defend myself."

One time during the night a large bear must have passed within about a quarter mile of the camp. The next morning Ada found its huge tracks near the traps. Its coming at night disappointed Knight because he had no chance to kill it. Finally, Ada found a female fox in a trap, and it provided a good meal for them and the cat.

Knight felt better after getting the meat. Because Ada was having to do more and more to care for Knight, she didn't always have time to go very far from camp to place traps; thus she caught fewer animals. Also daylight hours were still short, and Ada feared getting caught in the dark if she ventured too far from camp. On days that the traps were empty, the only food available was hard bread dipped in seal oil. Then one day their luck seemed to change. Ada had just gone outside when she turned and rushed back in, shouting that a bear was coming toward their camp along the beach from the east. The wind was blowing a little snow from the west and drifting along the ground. Knight told her to watch and when the bear got within about 200 yards to let him know. While she kept her eyes on the approaching animal, Knight stayed in his sleeping bag. Ada kept saying that the bear was getting closer and closer, but it had not arrived.

Knight thought it was taking the bear a long time to get to their camp, and he sent Ada to the roof of their house to look through his binoculars. When she got them focused, she realized that the "bear" was a yellow, dirty piece of ice in the distance. Seen through the drifting snow, it had appeared to be moving. Disappointment crushed both of them, and Knight continued to suffer from lack of meat.

In late February Ada began to show symptoms of what was probably scurvy. Her condition fluctuated from day to day. Some days she didn't feel like leaving the camp. Her spirits sank and for a while she seemed to lose her will to go on. Unfortunately, she did not share her own physical ailments with Knight, who mistook her symptoms for a return of the behavior she had displayed when they first arrived on the island. He wrote in his diary: "The woman says that she is not going to the traps any more and intimates

Arctic fox in white winter coat walking on snow.
Steven Kazlowski

she does not care whether we get any meat or not . . . says that she is ready to give up."

But Ada did check the traps the next day. Both their attitudes improved when she caught a fat female fox in one of the traps and prepared a tasty meal for the two of them and the cat. She barely cooked the meat in order to preserve the most vitamin C. After eating his fill of the fox meat, Knight felt somewhat better.

As March began, Knight's diary entries alternated between positive thinking and gloom. Ada caught one fox each day on the 2nd and the 3rd. Although they were scrawny, the two made welcome meals.

Arctic Fox

The Arctic fox has several adaptations that allow it to survive in the frigid places where it lives. Its compact 18- to 26-inch body exposes little skin to the air while its short muzzle, ears, and legs conserve heat. The fox wraps its brushy, 12-inch tail around its face to protect from cold winds. Its main protection is the deep, thick fur, which is also on its paws for walking on snow or ice. The fur changes color with the seasons—white in the winter in order to blend in with the snow and brown or gray in the summer.

The Arctic fox lives on the tundra, which for most of the year is bare and rocky without much vegetation. Therefore, the fox's main food is the lemming, a small rodent. Artic foxes are master hunters. They have a great sense of smell, incredible hearing, and wide, front-facing ears that allow them to locate the exact position of their prey in tunnels under the snow.

Mating season is from September to May, when the mother delivers a litter of 5 to 12 pups in a den in a hillside or bank with two entrances to provide an escape route if necessary. The male fox brings food to the mother and guards the den. He also helps to raise the pups.

Despite the intake of food, Knight expressed his frustration at his situation:

> Reading and lying on my back day-dreaming about "outside" to kill time, which goes rather slowly. It is bad enough to be laid up "outside" where one has newspapers, good food, a comfortable, clean bed and someone to talk to but I just lie here in my dirty hairy sleeping bag and read books again for the fourth or fifth time. As a conversationalist the woman is the bunk. Clear, calm and cold.

The very next day Knight was positive again, noting that Ada had caught a sizeable fox that provided them a big feed of almost raw meat. As the meat provided nourishment, he acknowledged feeling a little stronger. However, because of the heavy winds, Ada did not leave the camp to check the traps to replenish their meat supply. The next day she cut some wood and while doing some other chores, she broke the spade handle. Knight's final comment for the day was "All I want is to get a crack at a bear." No bears came, but Ada saw a lot of fox tracks across the harbor.

Knight's condition worsened. In a later interview recalling that time, Ada said, "It was a bad time. I don't like to talk about it." By March 9 Knight had lost the sense of touch in all his fingertips. His eyes watered when he tried to read or write. The craving for meat grew, but two days later he wrote that he could not swallow either hard bread or blubber. Hoping to catch some more foxes for soup, Ada set 12 traps. After she captured three foxes that day, she made soup, which Knight consumed hungrily. Getting fresh food had an almost immediate effect on his scurvy, and he slept better that night than he had for a long time. Ada continued to trap at least one fox a day, and Knight's entries repeatedly stated that he was feeling better. Ada decided to start her own diary because she had seen the men all write down what they did each day. Her entries were written in broken English with many misspellings. Her pencil was so dull that at times the words were scarcely legible. Still, she made her intentions clear: "My dary. I'm going write every day where I'm going so it will be easier to know what happen when Maurer Galle and Mr. Crawford come back. Today I'm going to the old camp. Might have chance to see seal . . . Well anyways I have to get some sweet roots."

Her earliest writings included information about her daily routine and her capture of animals, mostly birds and foxes, for food. Her writing was matter-of-fact with no trace of self-pity. Rather she recorded in a straightforward manner problems as they occurred. On March 14, she mentioned she had a headache and had taken aspirin, but it had not worked. Although she continued to feel unwell for several days with headaches and "stumpick [stomach] trouble," she rejoiced that Knight had told her she could keep his Bible. Days passed without incident as Ada mentioned chopping wood, washing her hair, and finishing a black belt she was making.

One morning the bear Knight had longed for finally appeared. But Knight was too weak to kill it and Ada had not yet learned to shoot the guns. However, she was glad to see signs of spring and welcomed the return from the south of birds like the snow bunting.

Even though the other three men had been gone almost two months, Ada still believed that they would come back. She knitted gloves for Galle, who had been her friend, so they would be ready when he returned. From an animal skin she cut new soles for her own slippers and skillfully sewed them on with sinew so that they would be water-proof. While she sewed, she watched Knight, dismayed at the downward progress of his disease. After finding 10 eggs in a seagull nest, she fixed them for Knight. He welcomed the tasty treat that replaced the meat he could not eat because of his sore throat, but he had become so weak that she had to hold up his head for him to take a drink of water.

Ada had no hot water bottle to relieve his pain so she made a canvas bag and filled it with hot sand to give warmth and comfort to his body, which by now was only skin and bones. She also sewed oatmeal sacks together and stuffed them with cotton that had been included in the supplies they brought with them to the island. She put the soft pillows under his thin shoulders and hips to ease his bed-sores. With the food they had brought almost gone, even crumbs became precious to the two. When she opened a new case of hard biscuits, Ada was careful not to lose any of the crumbs.

7

DOWNWARD SPIRAL

WITH THE APPROACH OF spring, conditions worsened for
the two survivors. A new scurvy symptom developed for
Knight: his gums began to shrink, causing his teeth to
loosen. He had difficulty swallowing, and his body, according to his own description, became "as thin as a side show
freak." Though his appetite was lessening, he forced himself to eat. Ada tried to provide as much meat as possible so
that he would get some needed vitamin C.

However, her chances of catching sufficient foxes were
decreased by an accident involving the traps and by her
own declining health. One night a fox got partially caught
in a trap and in trying to get free tangled itself in two more
traps, which it then dragged away. A few days later a sudden weakness overcame Ada, along with a sore throat and
pain and swelling in her eyes. She was battling both the
beginning stages of scurvy and snow blindness, causing

her to have to stay inside for three days. She wrote: "I didn't go out today because my face is swelen [swollen] and my eye is pretty near close from swelen and its very ach."

At times like these Ada wondered how she could go on. Thoughts of her little boy were all that offset her own sickness and weakness. She had to live for Bennett. She later revealed: "I said to myself I must stay alive—I will live—I will not let Bennett have stepmother."

Her illness scared her, and she thought she was going to die. In her diary she wrote about longing to go home and her wishes for her son: "If anything happen to me and my death is known, there is black stirp [strap] for Bennett school book bag, for my only son. I wish if you please take everything to Bennett that is belong to me. I don't know how much I would be glad to get home to folks."

Despite her fright she didn't tell Knight about feeling so bad. He wanted her to check the traps, but her eye hurt too much and she refused to go but didn't tell him why. She wrote in her diary, "knight [sic] wants me to go out to the traps but my eye is very ach so I cannot go out when my eye is that way because in evening I could bearly [sic] stand the ach of my eye and one side of head."

Since he didn't know she was sick, Knight thought she was being lazy and said some hurtful things about her refusal to work for a few days. Ada recorded his remarks in her diary: "And he menitions [mentions] my children and saying no wonder your children die you never take good care of them. He just tear me into pieces when he menition my children that I lost. This is the wosest life I ever live in the world."

Ada's scurvy symptoms receded and her eyes returned to normal. When she felt better, Ada went back outside to set traps, haul and chop wood, and look for eggs. She captured some geese. One goose had a large egg in its nest and the others two small ones. She also found a seagull egg. Knight ate some egg. He could no longer eat meat because of his loose teeth.

He had a long entry in his diary on March 23. Most surprising was the opening remark: "Caught myself whistling this A.M. Not that I don't want to whistle, God knows. However, this is in spirit only for I am as weak as a cat." He wrote that he had drunk a quart of fox soup, although fox made him queasy. He made optimistic comments about improvement in his gums, legs, and the red spots on his arms. Ada noticed that the color was returning to his legs, which had been bloodless. She continued to do her best to keep the two of them alive and to care for the ill Knight.

But sometimes the situation was almost too much for her. In one of his complaining moments, Knight blamed her for her marriage breakup. Ada wrote in her diary the cruel things Knight said to her: "He says Black Jack was good man and was right in everything and was right to tread [treat] me mean. And saying I wasn't good to him." In response to Knight's criticism, Ada wrote in her diary on April 21: "Its hard for women to take four mans place, to wood work and to hund [hunt] for something to eat for him and do waiting to his bed and take the shied [sheet] out for him."

Ada's diary became more and more a prayer on paper, with every entry ending with thanks to God. On Sunday,

April 24, with Vic wrapped around her feet and ankles, she recalled her life in Nome: "I didn't go out today. I just wash my hair and read the Bibil all day and think of folks are in church this morning and this evening and now I'm writing 11 o'clock in evening after I had cup of tea."

And again on the 30th, her dependency on God was clear: "This last day of April so knight is still living like anybody so if I happen to get back home I don't know much I would be glad God is the only one would brought me home again. There is no one pity me in this world but God even there is no hand would help me but God, with his loving kindness and mighty hand."

Gale force winds blew each day, forcing Ada to stay inside. On those days, Knight took out his frustration on her. However, one of her diary entries revealed her continued kindness to him: "Knight siad [sic] he was pretty sick and I didn't say nothing because I have nothing to say and he get mad and he through [throw] a book at me that secont [second] time he through book at me just because I have nothing to say to him. And I didn't say nothing to him and before I went in my sleeping bag I fell [fill] his water cup and went to bed."

Ada looked back at her earliest diary entries and marveled that she had written in the winter she would be glad if Knight lived until May. Here it was May and he was alive. Ada recorded her dreams—some encouraging, some not. In one she dreamed that she and Knight were all alone when he went to Siberia with a dog, leaving Ada by herself. She also dreamed about her and Bennett being with people swimming. Her loneliness was apparent in the next diary entry on May 8: "I wish was home so I hear people singing in Church. If the Lord only carry me home I will be there some day."

To help pass time, Ada made herself some seal skin boots and sewed on decorative beads to make this pair fancier than previous ones. May 10 passed without her mentioning that the date was her 25th birthday. Perhaps she failed to do so because she awoke that morning to a dripping sound. Her first response was that rain was leaking through the tent. As she became more awake, she glanced over at Knight and saw red all over his face. His nose was bleeding profusely into a one-pound tea tin. The can was almost half full.

Ada went to help him, but he turned his face from her. She called his name time and time again, but he had his back to her and refused to answer. Finally, he turned his head toward her and said that he was better. The nose bleed had started earlier, but he hated to admit his weakness and hadn't called Ada for help.

When she was not out hunting, she stayed beside his cot. Sometimes they talked; most of the time they didn't. Just having him there breathing—another human being— was a comfort to Ada, even though he could not help her in any other way. Usually at those times Ada sewed, making new boots, a parka, mittens, and a sunhat for herself. Sometimes she read to him from his grandfather's Bible. If the weather allowed, she went in search of food. If she couldn't find any meat, she brought back sweet roots that she boiled and made into a stew. One night she fried a biscuit for Knight. That was all he had eaten for nine days. He had become so thin that she did not believe he would live much longer.

In June Ada caught fewer and fewer foxes in the traps, but flocks of ducks arrived. In desperation, she decided she must learn to shoot a gun if she were going to get any food. Knight had forbade her to touch the guns, so whether he changed his mind or Ada did it surreptitiously, she made a target out of empty tea tins and started practicing.

The heavy gun bruised her shoulder with its sharp recoil, and, on the first try, she hit the target only twice. She felt pretty good about it though since she had never before shot with a .22 rifle. In between target practices, she dragged a 10-foot driftwood log to the camp, where she sawed half of it for fuel. She used some of the driftwood to build a little wooden rest for the gun barrel. By placing it on her shoulder, she didn't have to worry about the gun's weight, only about aiming it and pulling the trigger.

The next day she took four rifle shots at the target. The first three were from a sitting position, and she missed all of them. On her fourth shot she lay on her stomach and pierced the target right in the middle. Then she tried with the shotgun from a standing position, using the gun rest, and hit the target the first time. That night she made a shotgun cartridge bag and a case for a knife. She also took two pictures of the camp, although she didn't know much about using the camera.

By June 10, Ada no longer had any paper to continue her diary. Knight suggested that she write in a book of order blanks for photographic supplies. Her first entry could have served as a will:

... in case I happen to died or somebody fine out and found that I was dead I want **Mrs. Rita McCaffery** take care of my son Bennett. I don't want his father Black Jack to take him on a count of stepmother not for my boy. My sister Rita is just as good his own mother I know she love Bennett just as much as I do. I dare not my son have stepmother. If you please let this know to the Judge. If I got any money coming from boss of this company if $1200.00 give my mother Mrs. Ototook $200.00 if its only $600.00 give her $100.00 rest of it for my son. And let Rita have money enough to support Bennett.

She continued: "I just write noted in case Polar bear tear me down or case I fall in some rotten ice because I am hunding pretty near every day knight is very sick he hardly talk and he is skiny my he nothing but skin and bone as he lay in his sleeping bag for four months he pretty near die 10th of May and 12th."

Milton Galle had warned Ada not to touch his Corona typewriter, but when Knight's condition worsened she decided to risk his wrath in order to explain to him what had happened. This was her letter:

Dear Galle,

I didn't know I will have very important writing to do. You will forgive me wouldn't you. . . . I told you I wouldn't write with your typewriter. So I made up my mine. I'll write a few words, in case some happen to me because **Mr. Knight** he hardly know what he's talking about I guess he is going die he looks pretty bad. I hope I'll see you when you read letter. Well if nothing happen to me I'll see you. The reason why I write this important notice I have to go out seal hunding with the rifle. I was after seal on 18th of June. I shot two times to one seal but didn't hit the seal. And it was fogy so I think that's the reason why it's more hard for me to hit the seal . . . I didn't go out again because I didn't see anymore, but I try hard enough to get some eider duck. On 19th of June I got one female eider duck. Of course Knight wouldn't eat any meat he always say he's got sore throad. On 19th of June I found one seagal egg place and I found six more new nests and I saw bunch of seagals on one but didn't have any eggs. When I was coming back there was flock of geese but I took a shot there. One drip My! I was glad came home with one gees and after four days I went up again and I found nine eggs that is seagull eggs. Oh yes, the goose that I got had one egg and two smale ones the largest one had almost shell on it not quit through. That's about all I well say in this notice I write. I may write some more some times if nothing happens to me.

With lots of best regards to your self from me.

Yours truly

Mrs. Ada B. Jack

Knight grew weaker and weaker. His teeth fell out, and for two weeks all he could eat was broth. He bled constantly—his skin and his nose. The lack of vitamin C caused his capillaries to break down and just the pressure of lying down caused them to rupture. His bones were so brittle that he was afraid to move and lay on his cot like a statue. Ada later said: "He never complained. He knew he was going to die." His body sorely needed vitamin C. Unfortunately, he usually wanted Ada to fry the little meat they had because it tasted better to him that way. Of course, doing so prevented his getting the vitamin he needed, found only in raw or undercooked meat.

However, death was imminent, and Knight told Ada that when he died, she should put his diary and some other papers he had written in his trunk. He said that the key to the trunk was in his pants pockets. He also instructed her to keep his camera and his rifle dry. Shortly after he gave these instructions, he became unconscious. Ada stood,

Positive Effects of Vitamin C

The vitamin C from just a month of raw meat could have cured Knight's scurvy. The bleeding gums and nosebleeds would have disappeared within 24 hours. The capillaries bleeding into the skin would have healed in 48 hours, while the spots on the arms and legs would have disappeared in two weeks along with the muscle and bone pain. Most all the symptoms would have been completely gone at the end of the month.

looking down at him with tears streaming from her eyes. Knight rallied for just a minute to ask her, "What is the matter, Ada?" She told him that she feared his leaving her. She cried because she knew he could not last until the supply boat's arrival.

Despite Ada's best efforts at nursing Knight back to health, he died during the night of June 22–23, 1923. She found his body the next morning and documented his death in a note on Galle's typewriter in case she died before rescue:

Wrangel, Island
June 23d. 1923.
   The daid of Mr. Knights death He died on June 23d
I don't know what time he die though Anyway I write the daid [date]. Just to let Mr. Stefansson knew what month he died and what daid of the month

    writen by Mrs. Ada B, Jack.

Ada made a similar notation in Knight's diary. At the time she didn't notice a poem written by Knight and tucked into his diary. It summarized his last thoughts.

Knight's Poem

Here lies a Polar Explorer so valiant and bold
Who devoted his life to snowstorms and cold
All for prominence, so I've been told
And a few pieces of yellow filth called gold.
For nourishment he had snow and scenery

Which reminded him of the grim beanery
The grim beanery so greasy and grim
Would look like Paradise now to him.
Oh! Bring on your roast pork, apple sauce and pie
And some whipped cream before I die
Some of that wonderful potato salad, too
And sliced tomatoes with lots of goo-goo
And beans, Oh! Beans, that wonderful fruit
And then to end it all, just to make things suit
About a gallon of Mother's canned fruit
And then a wonderful bewitching smoke
For as tobacco is concerned I'm dead broke.
But I'm going now where it's always hot
Where blizzards ain't and cold is not
Where everyone's happy and anthems ringing
But having no voice I'll be out of the singing
Don't weep for me now, don't weep for me ever
I'm going to do nothing for ever and ever.

Knight was too big for the petite Ada to bury, so she left him wrapped in his deerskin sleeping bag that was on top of a narrow canvas cot. Then she used stacks of boxes to build a barrier at the tent's entrance to protect his body from marauding animals. She moved all of her own possessions to the other tent. Her diary entry that day simply summarized these actions: "I move to the other tent today and I was [wash] my dishes and getting some wood." She wrote nothing in her own diary about Knight's death.

With a strong spirit, Ada took steps to care for herself as long as she could. She stayed positive as noted in this entry on the 26th: "I found three see gall eggs in one nest. And cook them for my lunch I take tea and saccharine I had a nice picknick all by myself."

Ada strongly believed the other three men would return, although she didn't expect to live long enough to see them. However, she never doubted that they would come back to continue their Arctic research on Wrangel. In the meantime, she prepared for emergencies. On Galle's typewriter, she typed one more short note that she placed in an empty tube that once held photo developing powder: "Hello, somebody! This important notice is to say that Knight is daid and I with my kitten is all alone please send somebody to get me. (Signed) MRS. ADA BLACKJACK." For some reason she left the tube on the floor of the tent.

Except for the expedition cat, Vic, Ada was alone, at least 60 days walking distance to civilization in any direction.

Each time she went out to check the traps, Ada feared meeting a polar bear and ending up as its dinner. She wrote in her diary each day, with several entries detailing her search for and successful capture of some eider ducks. She became so accurate that she shot one duck through its head.

On the 28th she noted her continuing fear of polar bears: "This afternoon I hear some funny noise so I look out thought the door and saw Polar bear and one cub. I was very afraid so I took a shot over them see if they would go so they went away and they were looking back and I shot five times and they run away. I thank God that is true living God."

Later, when she was asked why she could shoot a duck's head but could not shoot the much larger polar bear, she replied: "When I shoot eider duck, my gun stays steady; but when I shoot at polar bear, my gun shakes in big circles."

Ada made a calendar out of small strips of typing paper to mark the passage of time in 1923. She used the dates to keep track of her diary entries. She also erected a crude framework of driftwood high above the back of the tent so that she could climb up to see farther distances without having to venture outside the camp. Its construction was not easy. She dragged boards and placed them on four uprights to which she nailed the planks. In front of the tent, she placed a small cupboard she made of boxes to hold her ammunition and her field glasses. With all the work she wore out the fingers of her gloves and had to knit new ones.

When birds and seals arrived, she made a little boat so she could get anything she shot in the water. She used pieces of driftwood to form the boat's bottom. She used as little wood as possible to keep the boat light enough for her to drag it across land and for it to sit high in the water. Because she did not have enough skins, she covered the frame with canvas stretched across the wood. She then sewed the canvas pieces together until a boat shape appeared. She also carved some driftwood oars to propel her little craft.

With the boat, she was able to pursue seal hunting with vigor. Her exuberance at getting one was reflected in her diary that day: "I got a seal. I shot it with the rifle. Oh I was glad when I got the seal and when I come home I cut the seal and hang the meat to dry." For an Eskimo, a seal meant everything—food, oil for lamps, and skin for clothing.

On the 4th of July Ada had an unsuccessful day of hunting. She crawled across the ice on her stomach to get close enough to shoot a seal. But as she aimed the gun, the seal moved and caused a big piece of ice to move between it and Ada, blocking her view. She shifted to get a better aim and accidentally pulled the trigger. The gun went off and the noise caused the seal to dive below the water. Ada lost her meat. Showing she had not lost her sense of humor, she wrote in her diary that day: "Boam [boom] it went and the seal went down and I stand up and say fourth of July." At that time Ada had been alone for 12 days.

Ada with the cat Vic, her only companion on Wrangel Island after Knight's death. *Courtesy of Dartmouth College Library, Rauner Special Collections*

8

RESCUE!

Ada's next search for a seal turned into a frightening experience. She crawled some distance to where the seal was sunning, took careful aim, and fired. The bullet found its mark and the seal died instantly. However, it was near its breathing hole and, although dead, its weight caused it to start sliding back into the water. Ada threw aside her rifle and raced as fast as she could over the uneven surface of the ice to grab the seal, which had already slipped near the ice floe's edge.

As she grasped the animal's flipper, she sensed a presence and looked over her shoulder. There stood a huge polar bear that had apparently been stalking her while she stalked the seal. Ada forgot about getting fresh meat and ran the 400 yards toward her tent. Fortunately, the bear did not chase her because it was enjoying the seal she had shot. Back in her tent, Ada climbed on the high platform at the back and used the field glasses to watch the bear. She later wrote in her diary: "I am glad it is not me polar bear eats."

The next day Ada shot two seals, hauled them to the tent, skinned them, hung the meat to dry, and stretched the skin. She concluded that day with: "All done at one day and this evening I took a bath. I thank the Lord Jesus."

A short time later, Ada had another encounter with the dreaded polar bears. She heard a noise like that of a dog just outside her tent door. She peeked out and saw, about 15 feet from the tent, a big bear and its cub. Ada said to herself: "What shall I do—what shall I do? If I shoot the mother bear and only wound her, she will get me—if I shoot her cub, she will be angry and eat me up—What shall I do?"

She decided to take a chance and grabbed the rifle. She knew that unless she could place a shot that would kill them, they would come after her. So she fired over their heads. They retreated a short distance. Then they turned around as if coming back. Ada fired five more shots in their direction, causing them to finally run away. Despite these frightening experiences, she wrote very little about the bears in her diary. She later explained the reason: "I do not write about bear in my 'dary' for if I die and someone reads my writings and my mother knows about it, she will always believe that I am eaten by polar bear, and in his stomach— no matter how I die, she will think polar bear eats me." In Eskimo beliefs, there could be no more horrible fate.

Meanwhile, unknown to Ada, the power boat *Donaldson*, commanded by Arctic explorer Harold Noice, had left Point Hope, Alaska, on August 9 and was trying to make its way to Wrangel Island.

The *Donaldson* making its way to Wrangel Island to rescue the expedition party. *Courtesy of Dartmouth College Library, Rauner Special Collections*

Twenty-seven-year-old Noice had accepted the challenge of getting a ship through the icy waters because he wanted to develop a reputation like that of Vilhjalmur Stefansson, with whom he had served on the Canadian expedition. He believed that bringing relief and supplies to the Stefansson party would add prestige to his own name.

Five hundred fifty-seven miles southeast of Wrangel Island, the *Donaldson* encountered an ice pack. The ship was sturdy, and with its new 65 horsepower engine it managed to break free after 10 days. Noice recalled that day: "I was at the masthead, high above the ice level, searching the white stretches for the zigzag leads of blue that are the navigator's only means of penetrating the great floes." A few days later, on August 19, Noice spotted a narrow lane of water on the east coast of the island.

There was a sigh of relief from the crew when the *Donaldson* got past the last cake of ice and entered that clear

The Donaldson

As Stefansson made plans to send supplies to Wrangel Island, he had difficulty in getting a ship. First, he lacked the funding needed for such a voyage but finally convinced his old friend Orville Wright to advance him the money. Wright was to be reimbursed by public and private donations, which Stefansson was still seeking. Stefansson heard about the *Donaldson*, owned by another friend, Alexander Allen, who was willing to rent his 72-foot-long motor schooner for a reasonable fee. Allen offered to hire a crew for the ship and to furnish sufficient supplies to meet their needs. He also agreed to provide enough engine oil and coal to run the boat, which would be completely outfitted and ready to sail by August 1923.

A separate concern for the *Donaldson* was a threat by the Soviet government, which claimed it was sending a gunboat to protect that nation's claim to Wrangel Island. Ignoring the Russians, Noice sailed the *Donaldson* from Nome on August 3. Depending on the sea conditions, he expected the ship to reach the island in two weeks. If, however, the ship became icebound, they would wait as close to Wrangel as possible while some of the men went by sled to check on the explorers' situation.

stretch of water bordering the island. The passage had been rough, and the sharp ice broke through the bow. They later repaired the hole by placing a large walrus skin over it. Noice and his crew arrived in the area during the short nighttime when the island's mountains seemed grim and forbidding. They could not see through the thick fog, and pessimism and gloom again filled the hearts of the crew and the Eskimo families they had brought to settle on Wrangel. They feared they had missed the island. "It was midnight when the fog suddenly lifted and there, stark black against the purplish sky, the cliffs of Wrangel rose like a forbidding wall across the ship's path."

Noice edged the ship along the coastline of the island, searching for the five people. He and his first officer had been on duty all night, and none of the other passengers and crew had gone to bed, although some of the Eskimos dozed among the deck's clutter—umiaks, sleds, and 20 shaggy haired dogs. With the dawn the view changed to reveal the whole shoreline of gravel and sandy beaches, replacing the dark mountains that now overlooked an expanse of moss-covered land. The crew felt optimistic again.

Suddenly a herd of walrus appeared near the edge of an ice pack. They roared and grunted as if protesting the boat's presence in their waters. The Eskimos cheered because they worried about the food supply when they were away from their home territory. Walruses were important food for them, so several jumped into an umiak and took off in pursuit. They shot two and towed the carcasses toward a nearby ice cake to wait for the *Donaldson* to catch up with them.

They loaded the animals on the ship while the other Eskimos chanted the walrus song. With this festive background, the ship chugged farther along the coast at dawn, searching for the party they were supposed to rescue. Those who had no other task served as lookouts in all directions. Suddenly fog again covered everything, and the shore faded to a shadow. Noice ordered the crew to cut the engines' speed while the ship moved closer to shore in order not to miss the people as well as avoid getting stuck on a sand bar.

Suddenly, a low cliff loomed out of the darkness and fog, a cliff that formed the northern boundary of Rodgers Harbour, where the expedition had landed two years ago. Noice anchored the ship, and he and some crew members went ashore in a skiff to investigate. They found no evidence of anyone having been there recently so they returned to the ship. They continued to nose along the coast for roughly 10 miles until they saw a dory drawn up on the beach about 40 yards from the water. Again the *Donaldson* stopped, and Noice, with some crew members, paddled ashore with mixed emotions. They wondered if the next discovery would be good or bad news.

They reached the beach, where they found signs that people had lived there, although there were no footprints or other evidence that they had been there recently. There were two abandoned camps with traps, snow knives, dog packs, and axe handles littering the ground. Noice assumed that this must have been the original camp site. Lying on the ground was a long pole with guy ropes attached to the top, probably used as a signal mast before winds had blown it over.

Near it they found a small oblong box covered with mud. Inside it was a bottle sealed with tallow. Inside the bottle was the Wrangel Island proclamation of ownership for Great Britain. It showed that the expedition had been there but gave no clue as to where they had gone. Noice was especially eager to find Lorne Knight. The two had first met when they served as crewmen on the *Polar Bear,* the ship that had picked up Vilhjalmur Stefansson on Cape Kellett after he had been presumed dead. As Knight and Noice became better acquainted with the famous explorer, Stefansson had invited both men to join his Canadian expedition.

Now the discovery of the proclamation spurred Noice and the others to search for a cave or a marker that might lead them to Knight and the rest of the party. Disappointed but still hopeful, they returned to the *Donaldson* and continued along the coast, where fog hung like a wet blanket. They stopped frequently to investigate every mound, and they blew the ship's whistle constantly. As they neared Doubtful Harbour in the early morning on August 20, they saw something moving on the beach. Noice wasn't sure whether it really moved or was a figment of the fog.

The morning before, Ada had awakened to find that during the night polar bears had eaten a full can of seal blubber that she had left just outside the door of her tent. Realizing how close the bears had come to her, she determined to be more careful so her meager supplies would last all winter. That evening, Ada heard a funny noise that sounded like a duck. She looked out the tent, but the weather was too foggy to see anything. Unable to go to sleep, she read for a while before going to bed. During the night she dreamed she heard a boat whistle.

The next morning about 6:00 AM, after fixing a meager breakfast of tea, dried duck, and seal oil, she wrote what turned out to be her last diary entry: "I finished my knited [sic] gloves today and I open last biscuit box, the ice is over little below horizon. I thank the lord Jesus and his father."

As she closed her diary, she heard the strange noise again, stronger this time although muffled by the fog. She grabbed the field glasses and climbed to the top of the platform. To her surprise she saw a boat in the water and a small skiff holding several people paddling toward the beach.

Ada could not believe her eyes. Half laughing and half crying, she darted across the beach and splashed through the shallow water, her hands stretched out, begging for help. She was dressed in furs, a faded snow shirt over a reindeer parka. A pair of field glasses swung from one shoulder. She pushed back the wolf skin fringe of her reindeer hood to meet her rescuers, Commander Harold Noice and the crew of the *Donaldson*.

Noice later reported:

I sprang out and shook her hand. For a moment neither of us spoke, and then she said: "Where is Crawford and Galle and Maurer?" and when I told that I had just arrived from Nome and expected to find them all on Wrangel Island she choked back a sob and said: "There is nobody here but me; I am all alone. Knight, he died on June 22." Then Ada, a queer,

frightened note in her voice, said, "I want to go back
to my mother. Will you take me back to Nome?"

When the commander assured her that he would take
her home, her face brightened for a moment and then she
fell forward, sobbing like a little girl. Noice broke her fall,
lifted her into the skiff, and took her to his cabin aboard
the *Donaldson*. He gave her a cup of hot coffee followed
by some breakfast. Somewhat revived, she told him her
story, beginning with the three men's preparation to walk
to Siberia for help:

> I don't know—much—how they went away. When they
> were loading up the sled, I was inside the tent, cry-
> ing, and then after they go, it blow wind with plenty
> snow drifting, and I think they get lost, or may be
> break through thin ice, but every time before I go
> to sleep I read my Bible and then I pray to the Lord
> Jesus to make them come back safe, and then when
> I see your ship I so glad, and I think you have those
> with you, and they are not lost, but now I guess they
> are gone all right, and I won't see them any more.

Every so often, she paused and said: "I wonder if this is
only a dream. I can hardly believe that you have come."

Noice had also brought the Eskimo families with him to
stay on Wrangel and continue its occupancy. He knew that
he would have to get the tent area cleaned up and dispose
of Knight's body before they would come ashore. He and
the crew headed back to land, with Ada reluctantly leading

them over the graveled beach in a fog that hung over the island like a ghostly shroud. Approaching the two flimsy tents, she indicated the smaller one was hers. Then pointing to the larger one, she told Noice: "Knight—he dead man now—him stay inside over there. Better we go first in my tent."

Outside the door to her tent, they saw a small canvas boat, crudely built but seaworthy. With pride, Ada told Noice she had made it, "After Knight die and birds and seal come I work hard to make a little boat so can get anything I shoot in the water. But only use it maybe two times when wind blow it away out to sea while I sleep. Then I cry all day and next day and next day, then I say to myself no use to cry any more, then I make this one, and now tie it up after every time I use it."

The furnishings inside the tent were meager. To the left of the door stood a rusty kerosene stove and a little pile of firewood. She explained that she had made the stove herself by cutting pieces out of old cans and hammering them together. Near the stove was a small box on which sat a battered teakettle. The box contained all the food she had left—some hard bread and a few pieces of dried meat. Against the back wall was the platform she had built from driftwood and empty crates covered with reindeer skins. To keep them dry, the shotgun and the rifle hung suspended from a rack overhead.

Ada's tent was cold because mist and fog drifted in through the ripped cloth. In this environment she had slept, eaten, hoped, and waited, always praying that help would come. Now she busied herself, lighting a fire and offering tea to Noice while he sat on a box and looked around. Suddenly Vic, the gray cat, emerged from behind some boxes and went to Ada, who picked it up and caressed it. As she held the cat, Ada told Noice a little more about Knight's last days: "All he could eat was sometimes a little soup—and by and by—I—I could not save his life—no matter how hard I try—he die and then me and Vic we moved over here in this place." Ada added that she thought she would have gone insane if she hadn't had the cat as a companion.

When it was time to go to the bigger tent, Ada stopped halfway there. Her lips trembled and tears flowed. She did not want to go where Knight's body lay. Noticing her reluctance, Noice told her to go back to her own tent and wait for him there. Outside, he found rusty trunks, tin boxes, boots, mittens, socks, knives, and files scattered all over the ground. Intermingled with all of these were torn pieces of wet deerskin that smelled of mold from long exposure to rain.

Then he and his men removed the box barricade Ada had built to keep out animals. On a narrow cot they found Knight's body with his head protruding from his deerskin sleeping bag just as it had been when Ada closed the eyes of the dead man two months earlier. Noice later said that although he thought he was prepared, it was "impossible to realize that this parchment-colored skull and inert skeleton could have once belonged to that happy, careless young giant who was the comrade of my early exploring days." Across the room was another cot, where Ada had slept all the months that she cared for the dying Knight.

Like the outside ground, the floor was littered with books, magazines, tattered volumes of Harvard classics,

and crumpled old periodicals filled with data. Mixed in
with all of these were unwashed dishes and dirty clothes.
In a corner stood a rusty stove whose pipe had tumbled
down, leaving a long tear in the canvas. Next to the body
was Knight's diary. Noice sat down on an empty cartridge
box and read for an hour.

The entries confirmed Ada's assertion that there had
been ample game available at first. The problem had been
with the men themselves, victims of a spirit of adventure
and youth and not prone to plan ahead. Their lives had been
pitted against untamed elements, and the struggle required

Cross marking site of Lorne Knight's burial on Wrangel Island.
Courtesy of Dartmouth College Library, Rauner Special Collections

leadership. Not one of the men realized the enormity of their task. They left Nome without sufficient food, failed to take Eskimo hunters with them, and didn't purchase the umiak for walrus hunting. Ada's later ingenuity in making a boat and a kerosene stove contrasted sharply with the men's inaction.

On August 21, 1923, almost two months to the day since he died, Lorne Knight was buried. Noice and his men built a coffin, lined it with white canvas, and made a white wooden cross to mark the grave site. They placed Knight's emaciated body in the coffin and carried it to the grave they had dug. Ada followed at a distance. Following some brief comments, the little ceremony was over in a few minutes. It was six o'clock. They had four hours of daylight to get the camp cleaned.

The rusty trunks held little because the three men had taken their diaries and maps with them, leaving behind a few loose sheets of notes, several packets of letters Maurer had written to his wife, and letters Crawford and Knight had written to Stefansson. They also found several cases of ammunition, an abundance of woolen cloth, and 17 unused deerskins. For the expedition members' parents, Noice collected a few keepsakes, including Knight's ring and watch. Then he and some of his crew pulled down the tents.

While the men worked, Ada went to her tent and packed her few belongings in an old suitcase. Among them was her little diary, sewn together with white cotton thread. After that, she sat on a box waiting and stroking Vic. On the floor around her were empty tubes that once held developing powder for pictures. It was into one of these tubes that

Ada had earlier stuffed her cry for rescue, although she had never tossed it into the ocean.

The Eskimos and others of the crew were busy unloading the boat. The lesson about insufficient supplies had been learned, and although the families were scheduled to stay only one winter on Wrangel Island, they had brought enough for two years. Ada recognized some of the crew members as men she knew from Nome. She immediately asked them for news of her son, Bennett. They assured her he was fine.

The *Donaldson* had brought mail for the expedition party, but there was only one letter for Ada. It was from a friend. Ada had hoped for letters from her sister telling her about Bennett. Ada so missed her young son's constant talking and his innumerable questions. He loved to tell even strangers about his life in Nome. She recalled the last time she had heard him tell such a story: "I have a reindeer; I can ride on his back—when I want him to go fast, I slap him with hand and he will run very fast so I have to hold on to his horns." His imagination fascinated Ada, but she wondered why he asked so many questions.

The twelve Alaskan Eskimos and one American, Charles Wells, would remain on Wrangel Island to continue claim to the island by occupation. Since they were all Americans, it was not likely that they would continue to claim it for Britain, but Stefansson had given up on getting any support from Great Britain or from Canada. However, the new settlers on Wrangel were still inspired by Stefansson's vision of a northward-moving civilization and of a Wrangel Island that would never again be unpopulated.

Ada waiting for Noice and crew to finish going through the big tent,
cleaning up, and seeking information about the expedition.
Courtesy of Dartmouth College Library, Rauner Special Collections

Wrangel Replacement Team

Charles Wells of Uniontown, Pennsylvania, and a group of 12 American Eskimo trappers lived on Wrangel Island for 12 months after Ada's rescue. During that time they collected a cache of furs they planned to sell. They never got a chance to do so because on August 20, 1924, the Soviets made a move to take over Wrangel Island, which they claimed they owned already.

Under the leadership of Russian Captain B. D. Davydov, the *Red October*, a gunboat, landed on the island with a cannon and a company of infantry men. Believing that the ship was their supply boat, the colonists eagerly paddled out to meet it. As Wells approached the boat, he saw the Russian hammer and sickle on its flag and knew he had made a grave mistake. The Russians confiscated the Americans' gear and the $10,000 worth of furs they had collected. After raising the Soviet flag on Wrangel Island, the Russians took all of the men prisoner and transported them to Vladivostok, Davydov's home port not far from Russia's borders with China and North Korea.

A few months later Charles Wells's captors announced that he had died of pneumonia. The Eskimos were moved to Manchurian China until arrangements were made for their transportation home. The

American Red Cross eventually wrote a $1,600 check to the Chinese and brought the Eskimos to Nome, Alaska. By that time, Russia had officially claimed Wrangel Island as Soviet territory, which it remains today.

Noice and his crew collected all that they could from the campsite—diaries, notes, scraps of paper, letters, and a few scientific reports. Then, along with Ada and Vic, they headed back to Nome. Noice later explained his feelings as he took the young heroine home:

I looked at her. How little she seemed—what pluck she had! I, who had long since ceased to believe in hero worship found myself unconsciously a little thrilled by the quality of her spirit. Alone, there on the island, down almost to her last morsel of food, Ada B was making ready to toss her pathetic appeal for help into the sea and entreat the waves to carry it safely to an inhabited shore.

At this point the man who had saved her also championed her.

As the *Donaldson* made its way homeward, Ada wrote about her ordeal, especially Knight's death. "I had hard time when he was dying. I never will forget that all my life. I was crying while he was living. I try my best to save his life but I can't quite save him."

9

CONFLICT AND CONFUSION

ADA STOOD ON THE deck of the *Donaldson* as it neared Nome with her eyes fixed steadily on the shore. Her quiet demeanor belied her excitement at once again seeing her son. When the ship docked, her sister Fina, along with her family, came on board to escort Ada home. Her sister Rita, whom Ada had named as Bennett's guardian should she die, tearfully embraced her.

As the family made their way through the streets of Nome, Ada talked a little about her feelings regarding her two-year ordeal. She assured her family that she held no resentment against Stefansson or Marshal Jordan, who had initially told her about the expedition. She freely admitted that no one forced her to go to Wrangel Island. Her only concern now was to get eight-year-old Bennett out of the Jesse Lee Home for Children. From her family, she

Ada, wearing the reindeer parka she made, stands on the deck of the *Donaldson*. *Courtesy of Dartmouth College Library, Rauner Special Collections.*

learned that her ex-husband, the abusive Jack Blackjack, had drowned in a river during the time she was gone. While Ada reunited with her family, Noice sent a telegram to Stefansson, notifying him of the loss of his expedition party and letting him know that the only survivor he found on the island was Ada Blackjack.

The arrival of Noice's telegram with news of the expedition's failure shocked Stefansson, who was in England when he received it on September 1, 1923. He sent brief condolences by telegram to all the families except the Galles, a strange omission considering the fact that Galle had once been Stefansson's secretary and that he and the Galles had corresponded several times during the two years. To the Maurers Stefansson wrote: "Sympathy to you all and Fred's wife." He provided no further information. Maurer's brothers, John and Thomas, refused to accept the initial news of their brother's death. He had previously survived six months on Wrangel Island following the *Karluk* incident, and they believed that he was probably safe somewhere on the Siberian coast. They petitioned the US government to send out a search party, but to no avail.

The Crawfords first heard the news of their son Allan's death when a *Toronto Star* reporter contacted them. Crawford's father, Professor J. T. Crawford, simply remarked, "This is terrible news." He said that he had received no word from his oldest son except for the initial letter carried back by the *Silver Wave* notifying the family of his arrival on Wrangel Island. That letter, the last words they ever had from their son, ended, "Love to you all, good-bye to you all till next year: Alan [*sic*]."

As soon as Stefansson's telegram arrived in McMinnville, Oregon, before dawn, a policeman friend of the
Knight family brought the crushing news to them. Mr.
Knight notified Lorne's girlfriend, Doris Jones, but his main
concern was to get his son's body back for a proper burial.
He could not understand why Noice had not contacted the
Knights about that, so he and his other son, Joseph, made
plans to meet the passsenger ship *Victoria* when Noice
arrived in Seattle, assuming Knight's body would be on
board. While he waited, John Knight wrote a letter of sympathy to the Galle family because he had encouraged them
to let their young son go on the adventure, assuring them
that he would be safe. When the ship arrived on September
17, Knight was devastated to learn that his son's body was
not on it. Noice tried to pacify the grieving father by giving him his son's last letter but refused to give him Lorne's
diary, claiming that it had to first be copied by the expedition commission.

In Texas, Harry and Alma Galle, having received no
telegram from Stefansson, first heard the news about their
son Milton from a relative, Joe Abrahams, who saw the
headlines on September 1 in the New Braunfels newspaper. Then the parents had the difficult task of telling Galle's
younger brother and sister, both of whom were students
at the University of Texas in Austin. However, the family never fully accepted Milton's death, refusing to give up
hope.

A few weeks after the families received notification of
their sons' deaths, news of three white men seen wandering
along the Siberian coast raised the hopes of the distraught

families. They encouraged themselves with thoughts of how Captain Bartlett had led the *Karluk* survivors across the ice in 1914. They speculated. Perhaps their loved ones had taken a wrong turn in their wanderings and had not yet reached a wireless station to send a message about their safety. Because of the language difference, they would be unable to communicate with the Eskimo groups that lived along that far north land. Another possibility was that they had been temporarily captured by Russians.

This idea sent a flurry of requests to all levels of government and to the international Red Cross to send out a relief boat. Replies from government agencies and various congressmen were all negative. The families were told it was not the right time to send a relief boat—there was too much ice. By the first of October all ports would be icebound. All their ideas turned out to be only frustrated hopes; no rescue was launched.

In October Stefansson arrived back in the United States. He learned from his business associate, Alfred J. T. Taylor, that Noice had refused to let him see Lorne Knight's diary. Instead Noice had tried to negotiate with Taylor to use that journal and Ada's diary in his own writings. Noice claimed that the papers belonged to him. Already he had started releasing information from Lorne's diary to newspapers. Most of the articles painted Stefansson in a bad light, claiming that he had not sufficiently prepared the young men for their expedition.

As more information about the failed expedition was publicized, Stefansson faced a great deal of criticism from the public about the men's lack of preparation and the insufficiency of their supplies. Stefansson resented the implications that he was to blame for the tragedy, and he wanted to read the diaries for himself. In New York he met Noice, who insisted the men's incompetence and inadequate supplies led to their deaths. He also believed they lacked leadership and that Stefansson should have gone with them.

Stefansson was furious. Such accusations challenged his belief that the Arctic was a friendly place, where white men could easily survive by following Eskimo ways. To add to his troubles, he was getting complaints from the British, Canadian, and American governments about his attempts to claim Wrangel Island. As a speaker on the Chautauqua circuit, where he told adventure stories about the Arctic, these accusations would be damaging. He demanded to see the diaries. He read through them and other papers Noice had collected on the island.

Much to Stefansson's surprise, he found large sections of Knight's diaries had been ripped out. In other places there were heavy strikeovers and erasures that completely blurred the wording. Noice claimed he had received the diaries in that condition, hinting that Ada had done the damage. In the meantime he continued to feed negativity to the newspapers. An angry Stefansson started answering the charges, and the two men carried on a war of words.

Ada wanted to avoid reporters and disappeared for a while to the disappointment of the men's parents who wanted to hear the story from her directly. The Galles had not received a final letter from their son as had the other three families. They wrote to Stefansson, asking about such a message. He had a secretary reply to them that there was not such a letter probably because "he [Milton] was full of hope and thought it unnecessary."

As always, Ada's main concern was not the feuding of the two men but her son Bennett's health. While Stefansson dealt with the press and the young men's families, in early November she went to Seattle, where one of her sisters and her husband lived, but Ada decided that she and Bennett would stay in a hotel instead of with her family. Everything about the city scared Ada. At first she refused to ride in the hotel elevator but overcame that fear. For several days, she didn't want to leave her hotel room. When she finally ventured out, the traffic scared her. She walked around the block for exercise, always keeping the hotel in view so that she would not get lost.

As her confidence grew, she ventured farther away from the hotel. She had always liked clothes and so she went shopping. She had only $20 to spend but managed to purchase a dark suit, two cotton blouses, a straw hat, and a suitcase. When she started to pay, she realized she was short 10 cents. The clerk told her not to worry about it. Her other outings were often to the theater to see films, which she and Bennett both enjoyed.

After she had been in Seattle for a little while and learned her way around the city, she sought medical help for Bennett's tuberculosis and got him placed in a hospital for treatment. While he was there, Ada lived in a run-down shack, trying to save her money for Bennett's treatments. It was at this hovel that Lorne Knight's father finally found her. He wanted to talk to her to hear about his son's last days.

Communication was difficult. Mr. Knight did not know that before Ada left for Wrangel someone had advised her not to sign anything, probably referring to contracts, and not to answer questions. Ada had promised. A promise was important to her, so she was still observing her pledge not to talk.

She spent only 10 minutes with Mr. Knight, despite his long trip from Oregon to see her. However, Ada's dignity and quiet explanations impressed him. He wanted to hear more and invited her to come visit him and his wife in Oregon. Although reluctant to travel to one more place unfamiliar to her, Ada agreed to go while Bennett was safe in the hospital. She felt she owed it to the Knights to tell them about their son's last days.

On December 10, Ada traveled by train to Portland, Oregon, where the Knights met her at the station. She had her first ride in a car when they traveled the 40 miles from Portland to McMinnville. Ada had agreed to stay with the Knights until Christmas if Bennett continued to do well in the hospital. The morning after her arrival she took Lorne's Kodak camera and the Bible he had given her out of her suitcase. Even though he had told her she could keep the Bible, she felt under the circumstances that she should return it to his family. When they saw how much she treasured the Bible, they assured her Lorne would have wanted her to keep it.

A steady stream of the Knights' friends and other visitors came to the house. Although they were curious about Ada, most were respectful and truly interested in her story. A few, however, treated her like a wild woman—one person even suggested she was a cannibal.

Kodak Camera

On May 1888 a dramatic event occurred in America's history—the invention of a camera that ordinary citizens could operate. It cost $25, a great deal of money at the time, but it was easy to use. George Eastman, its inventor, created the slogan: "You press the button, we do the rest."

Americans pressed the button and Eastman raced to keep production equal to demand. Notable people like President Grover Cleveland had a Kodak, but he usually forgot to turn the key that advanced the film for the next picture, causing double exposures and poor pictures. Opera composers Gilbert and Sullivan wrote a song about the Kodak for their operetta *Utopia*.

As with any new invention, there were problems. A man who dubbed himself the "camera fiend" went to public beaches, where he snapped photos of unaware women in their swimsuits. As a result, cameras were banned on many beaches and at the Washington Memorial.

It was a time of change in America—more and more automobiles were seen on the streets, and ordinary citizens had the new telephone in their homes. Kodak snapshots allowed Americans to share their good times beyond the moment.

From her first day with them, the Knights showered
Ada with gifts—an engraved watch, an American flag
that had belonged to Lorne, and her own Kodak camera.
The obvious concern she had shown for their son's welfare
impressed them, and they invited her and Bennett to come
live with them. They told her, "You are all we have left of
the Wrangle [*sic*] Island expedition, and we feel that you
are now almost a part of the family. We would be glad if
you would like it, to have you live with us so that we could
repay you for what you did for Lorne." Ada appreciated
the offer but declined, feeling that it would be a constant
reminder of that difficult time.

After not quite a week in Oregon, Ada received word
that Bennett had developed measles. The Knights drove
her to Portland on the 16th, and she rode the train back to
Seattle to tend to her son. Bennett stayed in the hospital
until the disease had run its course and was then released.
He still had tubercular lesions on his chest and neck and
was thin, pale, and weak. His doctor recommended that he
go to California, where his body could get direct exposure
to sunlight to complete his cure.

Stefansson came to Seattle, and he and Ada met several times. Although he had difficulty getting her to talk,
she did assure him that Lorne's diaries were complete and
had no erasures or marks on them when Noice took them
from Wrangel. During their conversations, Ada told Stefansson about Bennett's illness and his need for a climate
change. However, she didn't have enough money to make
such a trip. Stefansson introduced her to his friend, Mrs.
Inglis Fletcher. She had a son about Bennett's age who also

Ada Blackjack standing in front of Lorne Knight's family home when she visited his parents. *Courtesy of Dartmouth College Library, Rauner Special Collections*

suffered from illness. They were headed to Hollywood, California, to visit some friends who owned Strongheart and other wonder dogs of movie fame.

Strongheart, along with other movie dogs, was housed on a farm just outside Hollywood. Since Bennett loved the movie dogs, especially Strongheart, this would be a wonderful place for him to run and play, his skin exposed almost completely to the sun. Mrs. Fletcher agreed to take care of Ada and Bennett on the trip if Stefansson would pay their passage to California. Even though going farther away from home scared Ada, she agreed when she heard how the trip could benefit Bennett.

The trip established a deep friendship between the two women, and Ada confided to Mrs. Fletcher the story of her ordeal. As she listened to Ada, Mrs. Fletcher realized that it was Ada's love of Bennett that had kept her striving to stay alive on Wrangel Island no matter how difficult it was. It was her maternal instinct that made her determined to get back to Nome and now to venture to a strange state to help her son.

Mrs. Fletcher was the one who responded to reporters' calling Ada a female Robinson Crusoe. She argued that although Ada's situation was reminiscent of Robinson Crusoe, there was a major difference—Crusoe had his man Friday; eventually, Ada had only the cat Vic.

On the boat to California people wanted to hear Ada's story about Wrangel Island, but she was reluctant to recall that hard time because, as she said, "It always makes me have a choke in my throat and tears come to my eyes." She answered questions as briefly as possible, and when

Strongheart

The famous German shepherd Strongheart was born in Germany on October 1, 1917, and given the name Etzel von Oringer. Trained as a police dog, he served with the military during World War I. An American movie director was searching for a dog to use in movies. When he saw Strongheart, he knew he had found the right one. Because of his police dog training Strongheart had difficulty socializing, but he eventually became accustomed to people, although he seemed to have a sixth sense about those of low moral character.

His first movie, *The Silent Call*, endeared him to children and adults alike. He traveled widely to make public appearances and was always given star treatment and a huge welcome wherever the train stopped. Two books were written about him, and he appeared in five other films. He and his mate, Lady Jule, produced numerous litters. Two of their grandsons, Lightning and Silver King, became movie stars as well.

At the height of his career, Strongheart slipped and was burned by a studio light. The burn never healed, and the brave dog died on June 24, 1929. He was awarded a star on the Hollywood Walk of Fame for motion pictures.

reporters persisted, she and Bennett retreated to their cabin.

While Ada was in California, Noice turned against her. He retracted all of the complimentary things he had said when he first rescued her and now accused her of having killed Knight. One accusatory headline read: "Ada refused to aid E. Lorne Knight as he lay dying—saved herself on food that would have kept Knight from dying." Since Noice had initially provided the newspapers with the information about the Wrangel Island expedition, they assumed that his new outlook was correct and based on information that he alone had later found in Knight's diaries and the scattered papers of the other men. The press reviled Ada.

Noice's accusations appeared in large-type headlines in newspapers throughout Canada, Alaska, and parts of the United States. The February 12, 1924, issue of the *Vancouver Daily World* claimed "Eskimo Woman Blamed for Canadian Explorer's Death." The article claimed that earlier stories of her heroism had been based on her own words and her brief crude diary. From Knight's diary, Noice gathered information about Ada's refusing to take care of the traps near their tent and spending time washing her hair and making a bed for herself while Knight lay dying. Noice further asserted that when he arrived on the island, he found the dead emaciated body of Knight, whom he claimed had died of starvation. In contrast, he claimed Ada was plump and had plenty of hardtack, blubber, and tea stashed away for herself.

However, Knight's parents did not accept Noice's accusations. Based on their conversations with Ada when she visited them, they believed that she had done all possible to save their son. Hating the way Ada was being attacked by the press, Mr. Knight issued a statement to the papers: "I still maintain that Ada Blackjack is a real heroine, and that there is nothing to justify me in the faintest belief that she did not do for Lorne all that she was able to do . . . I feel that I owe [this statement] to the public and to a poor Eskimo woman who is being wronged and is helpless to defend herself."

For once Ada ignored her fear of reporters and went directly to a Los Angeles newspaper office, where she refuted Noice's charges with a simple explanation.

Knight was sick. He could not go out to hunt or trap. He thought I should do it. I didn't know how to trap. I was hired to sew skins as a seamstress. But I learned how to trap. I trapped fox for Knight and gave him all the tender pieces. I hunted gulls' eggs for him and fed them to him. I hauled wood for fires. With the work and anxiety I grew sick myself. For a month I could not make the rounds of the traps. . . Day by day he grew weaker. For the last two days he was unconscious. Before that while he still could talk he thanked me for what I had done for him. During the month while I was too sick to trap Knight was some times angry with me. I suppose he thought that I was shirking . . . For two months I was alone on the island with his body. Together we were many months alone there and at times both helpless from illness. It was hard. But these accusation are harder still. There is no truth to them.

The next morning the newspaper printed a sympathetic account of Ada's experience on Wrangel Island. She later explained how she got the courage to approach the newspaper office: "When I got to thinking about what they are saying about me, my throat chokes and tears run from my eyes like water in the river when ice melts, and I turn my face away and look out car window so no one will be seeing me—and I think I will walk up to newspaper and say a few words."

Pictures in newspapers revealed that Ada was not fat. This led to questions about why Noice had lied. For some reason, he had turned against Stefansson and planned to blackmail him with the threat of revealing scandals on the *Karluk* expedition that some believed Stefansson abandoned. Noice also wanted to publish a book about the Wrangel Island expedition and thought his accusations would be good publicity.

Stefansson eventually forced Noice to sign a retraction of all the falsehoods about Ada. Noice's excuse for his abominable behavior was a nervous illness. The written statement concluded with this: "I sincerely regret that any false impressions have been given and humbly apologize for my errors."

With all the conflicting reports, the families of Ada's four companions on Wrangel continued to search for answers about what had happened to their sons. Newspapers carried a flurry of speculations after Stefansson spoke about the situation, denying that potential starvation motivated the men. He argued that they had planned the trip for six months before actually making it. He failed to say that it was the first trip they planned several months in advance, but it was the second one that led to their deaths.

In reading some of their son's letters that had been retrieved, the Crawfords found this statement, which contradicted Stefansson's assertions: "When I saw how sparse seal and bear were I decided it would be unwise to stay here with the dogs all winter. Especially so since trapping is not worth staying for." The furious couple asked the *Ottawa Journal* to print their signed statement of resentment.

In addition to making misleading statements Mr. Stefansson indulges in callous and futile speculation as to what cruel death may have been the unknown fate of my son, Allan Crawford, and his two companions, Frederick Maurer and Milton Galle. He has endeavored to convince the public that their tragic end was a mere accident, that starvation could not have been its cause, although he himself has admitted that a supply for six months was all the food he advised them to take, and has stated in the *London Spectator* (August 18, 1923) that "their supplies probably gave out a year ago!"

After the Crawfords' published challenge to his veracity, Stefansson modified his approach in a letter to Mrs. Galle, explaining that one of two things could have happened to the men. They could have broken through the ice and drowned because the currents north of Alaska and north of Siberia were so strong that the ice was in continuous sluggish motion. The ice between the heavy cakes was, therefore, treacherously weak in places, for it was only a few days old.

> If you have a gale that breaks up the ice so that perhaps one-quarter of the surface of the sea is open water between floating cakes, then during the next two or three days new ice will form connecting these loose cakes and spreading over the water between them. This sort of young ice is not ordinarily dangerous except in the case of a heavy snowfall that not only blankets the ice, preventing it from getting thicker and stronger, but also conceals any weakness there may be. If the traveler is eager to make a long day's journey, he would probably travel not only through the five or six hours of good daylight we have in January in this latitude, but also an hour or two into the thickening twilight. If then the party comes to young ice that has been covered with a heavy fall of new snow, they may walk out on it if they are just a little careless, realizing no danger until everything gives way beneath them.

The other alternative he gave as he concluded the letter was that they could have been swept away by a strong wind. "During a cloudy and stormy night the party may be encamped on ice which begins to break under the influence of the wind and current." Another problem that he didn't mention was that the wind could also cause multiple ridges that were difficult, if not impossible, to cross. Knight had noted in his diary that on the day after the three left to walk to Siberia there was a forceful gale that blew through the camp. The same storm could have caught the men. Mr. and Mrs. Galle corresponded with Stefansson on an almost monthly basis for over a year, trying to make sense out of their son's fate. Stefansson wrote back with lengthy responses that seemed to make excuses more than answer their questions. Based upon what he read in Knight's diary, Stefansson assured the couple that their son was content on the island. In early 1924, he distributed copies of the diary to the families themselves. After reading it, the Galles commented to him that if Ada could catch enough food to keep her and Knight alive then the men should have been able to do the same. They further contended, "We fail to see why not enough [food] was taken to rather have some to spare than to run short, as the inaccessibility of the island was known."

For the longest time Stefansson claimed that the three men left the island not because of a food shortage but because of their desire to communicate with him. Therefore, he responded to the Galles:

I think you are right in saying that if Ada could catch enough game to keep her alive the three boys would have been able to do much better had they remained. That is undoubtedly true. Had safety been the only question, they would have all remained on the island, going on short rations during the darkness during the winter and then beginning to hunt energetically when the daylight came in February and March. Both Crawford's last letter to me and Lorne's diary show that they planned the trip to Siberia more than six months before they made it and that the original plan was not based on any expectation of scarcity of food but rather on their idea that it was what they ought to do in carrying out the general plans of the expedition as discussed between us before they sailed north.

In March 1924 the Galles finally received from Stefansson the scraps of paper that constituted Milton's diary as well as a typed copy. As they read the information retrieved from these papers, they pressed Stefansson for proof that Milton had been an equal member of the expedition. When they learned that he had not known about the men's plans to walk to Nome and then Siberia, they wanted to know if he did not get along with the rest of the team. Stefansson responded:

There are in one or two places evidence of slight friction but all those familiar with the confidential story of other expeditions will know that there scarcely ever has been so long a polar expedition with so little disagreement among the men . . . after all they were only misunderstandings, and if he was to blame at all it was only that he was too diffident to ask direct questions. I have no doubt but if he had asked directly, Crawford and Knight would have told him, for instance, just what their plans were for leaving the island and why they were going.

They continued to carry on the correspondence seeking more information, even though shortly after they received news of his death, Milton's parents had stopped speaking his name. His mother took down all of his pictures in their home. To this day, there is no marker for him in the family plot in Comal Cemetery because they had no body to bury. He is the only one of the four explorers not to have a monument in his honor.

Stefansson still needed to get Ada's permission to use her diary in the book he was writing about the Wrangel expedition. By then she was living in run-down rooms in Seattle, where Ingris Fletcher found her and Bennett in December 1924. Ingris was surprised to discover that Ada had a two-month old son, whom she had named Billy. Although Ingris was not sure who the father was, Billy eventually took the name of George Johnson, with whom Ada later had a brief marriage in 1928. Ingris had come to get Ada to agree to allow Stefansson the rights to her story and to swear in writing that she had not been the one to deface Knight's diary. He promised Ada that, if she granted him permission, she would receive royalties from his forthcoming book *The Adventure of Wrangel Island*, which was published in 1925. However, Ada never received a penny.

Meanwhile, she needed money to pay for medical care for Bennett, whose health was declining. To add to her troubles, she was walking with baby Billy one day when she slipped off a sidewalk into the street and was hit by a car. Although she and her son received only minor injuries, Ada believed the accident was a sign that she should leave Seattle. She planned to head to Spokane, Washington, where she believed she could get assistance from the Salvation Army. She used the last of her money to buy train tickets.

Nothing was heard about Ada for two years until a newspaper reported that Ada was suffering from tuberculosis and that she had once again put her sons in the Jesse Lee Home in Nome. By that time Bennett had developed spinal meningitis that caused deafness and blindness in one eye. Both boys learned sign language so that they could communicate with each other. Despite her illness, Ada married George Johnson, from whom she separated after a short time.

In October 1929, she took the boys out of the Jesse Lee Home and moved the family back to Seattle, where they lived for 14 years. To earn a living, Ada took on such jobs as herding reindeer and hunting and trapping. When Billy reached the age of 21, he enlisted in the army and served from 1945 to 1948. He was sent to Germany, where he met his future wife, Gisela Sperber.

After years of financial difficulty in Seattle, Ada returned to Anchorage. She later recalled, "I had a hard time in Seattle. There was no money, and I had to have surgery. The welfare people told me to get out and go to work. About the only work I could find was berry-picking in the summertime."

Following her return to Anchorage, Ada lived in a shack and combed the beaches for driftwood that she could sell to support herself. The money earned during her ordeal on Wrangel had long been spent. Among her few possessions was the Bible given to her by Lorne Knight. The rest of her life was a constant battle against poverty, illness, and embarrassment at the accusations cast against her.

Although Billy had his own family and interests, he helped his mother with the care of Bennett until his brother's death at age 58 in 1972. The Johnsons moved to Seattle and raised a large family. Billy was active in business and political groups and became a lobbyist for the 13th Regional Corporation, originally established by Congress to stimulate economic development and provide for the welfare of Alaskan natives.

Following a stroke that left her unable to speak, Ada Blackjack Johnson died in the Palmer Pioneer's Nursing Home on May 29, 1983, at the age of 85. She was buried at Anchorage Memorial Park Cemetery. After her death, Billy placed a large plaque on his mother's grave. It read: "Ada Blackjack Johnson, HEROINE WRANGEL ISLAND EXPEDITION, 1921–1923." But to him that was not adequate recognition for all that his mother had done.

He told reporters:

I consider my mother Ada Blackjack to be one of the most loving mothers in this world and one of the greatest heroines in the history of Arctic exploration. She survived against all odds. It's a wonderful story that should not be lost of ... a mother fighting to survive to live so she could carry on with her son Bennett and help him fight the illness that was consuming him. She succeeded, and I was born later. Her story of survival in the Arctic will be a great chapter in the history of the Arctic and Alaska. Time is running out, and soon this chapter will fade away unless we care enough to make a record of it.

A month after her death, the Alaska Legislature heeded Billy's admonition and officially recognized Ada's heroism. They issued a citation which was "a small token of remembrance for a woman whose bravery and heroic deeds have gone unnoticed for so many years." Billy died in North Carolina at age 78 in 2003. He was survived by his second wife, Janice Johnson, three daughters, five sons, one stepdaughter, 13 grandchildren, and one great-grandchild.

Ada Blackjack Johnson's life began in poverty and ended in poverty. In between she married twice, had four children, two of whom died in childhood, traveled to the desolate Wrangel Island, where she survived the deaths of her four expedition companions, came home to a heroine's welcome, only to be severely criticized and charged with murder by her rescuer. She not only was a master seamstress but showed other creative skills by building a kerosene stove and constructing two canvas boats while on the island.

On her own, she learned to shoot a shotgun and a rifle, how to set animal traps, how to skin, dissect, and cook those animals, and how to stretch her meager food supply to enable her to stay alive. Her ongoing motivation for all she did was the care of her first son, Bennett, who suffered from multiple illnesses. Ada Blackjack was an amazing woman who truly deserves the title "heroine of Wrangel Island."

AFTERWORD

WRANGEL ISLAND TODAY

FOR THREE-FOURTHS OF THE year, Wrangel Island is a lonely, bleak place of only three colors—black, gray, and white. In 1976 the Soviet government declared it a federally managed nature sanctuary. It has since become a natural laboratory for Arctic animals and those who study them with plans to develop a system to protect the polar bears, walruses, and snow geese that flourish on the island. Scientists who have gone there describe it as "the end of the earth" and a "pristine environment."

The island can be reached only by helicopter or by ship during the few summer months when ice does not hamper passage. But during those summer months the island becomes alive with daisies, forget-me-knots, and poppies blooming from the tundra. Polar bear mothers come by the hundreds to give birth to their cubs and to raise their young.

Since taking over the island from Charles Wells and 12 Eskimos in 1924, Russia at various times used it as a prison, a concentration camp for political prisoners, and as a KGB camp to train foreign agents. For the most part, official personnel and invited guests are the only ones allowed access to the restricted reserve, although in recent years it has become a stopping point for some cruises.

About 100 Eskimos live in the small village of Ushakovskoe, which serves as a base camp for an additional 30 seasonal reserve staff who work from field stations during all but the winter months. A weather station, an airstrip, a large meteorological station, and two small fishing settlements are on the southern side of Wrangel. Today it is one of Russia's most treasured wildlife sanctuaries. There is no reminder of the castaway Ada Blackjack and the island's doomed 1921–1923 expedition.

ACKNOWLEDGMENTS

THANK YOU TO Lynn Thompson, assistant director, New Braunfels Public Library, New Braunfels, Texas; the staff at Dartmouth College Library, Rauner Special Collections; and the East Carolina University Archives librarians.

NOTES

CHAPTER I: IN THE BEGINNING

"From the time we left": Milton Galle letter to Stefansson, September 8, 1921.

"a harsh environment": Josh Hilliard, "Arctic Images: Portraying a 'Friendly Arctic,'" www.dartmouth.edu/~library/digital/collections/photographs/ocn237336112/friendlyarctic.html.

"There is absolutely nothing": Noice, *With Stefansson in the Arctic*, 32.

"The returning party": "Sole Survivor Tells Tale of Arctic Party," *Carp Review*, September 13, 1923.

"When we got to Wrangel": Stefansson, *The Adventure of Wrangel Island*, 327–328.

"Know by all these": Stefansson, *The Adventure of Wrangel Island*, 118–119.

"in rather poor shape": Stefansson, *The Adventure of Wrangel Island*, 116.

MEET VILHJALMUR STEFANSSON

"*West of the Coppermine*": Gísli Pálsson, "The Legacy of Vilhjalmur Stefansson," www.thearctic.is/articles/topics/legacy stefansson/enska/index.htm.

CHAPTER 2: SETTLING ON THE ISLAND

"*Dear Mr. Stefansson*": Stefansson, *The Adventure of Wrangel Island*, 118–119.

"*A beautiful day*": "Explorer's Notes Tell of Busy Life in Artic but Are Tinged with Impending Tragedy," *Bridgeport Telegram*, October 31, 1923.

"*September 20: Busy digging out*": Stefansson, *The Adventure of Wrangel Island*, 182–183.

"*sewing clothing, and*": Stefansson, *The Adventure of Wrangel Island*, 182.

"*This morning Galle went*": Stefansson, *The Adventure of Wrangel Island*, 193.

"*Eight bears were seen*": Stefansson, *The Adventure of Wrangel Island*, 194.

"*The woman has had several*": Stefansson, *The Adventure of Wrangel Island*, 384.

"*All we need now*": "Life on Wrangel Like a Cooper Romance First Year," *Bridgeport Telegram*, November 1, 1923.

"*All hands went with a sled*": Stefansson, *The Adventure of Wrangel Island*, 195.

"*This may sound funny*": Hardy, W. F., "As I View the Thing: A Heroine of the Far North," *Decatur Herald*, May 13, 1931.

"*Supper is over*": "Life on Wrangel Like a Cooper Romance," *Bridgeport Telegram*.

MEET MILTON GALLE

"By now you have": Milton Galle letter to parents, August 15, 1921.

"To my thinking": Western Union telegram from Milton Galle to his parents, 1921.

CHAPTER 3: CHANGING WINDS

"December 21, 1921: Blowing a strong": "First Winter on Wrangel Island Was Like a Romance by Cooper; Polar Bears Plentiful and Often They Become Very Inquisitive," *Indianapolis News*, November 9, 1923.

"December 24, 1921: Galle Is Working": "First Winter on Wrangel Island," *Indianapolis News*.

"December 25, 1921: Spending the day": "First Winter on Wrangel Island," *Indianapolis News*.

"I went out to look": Stefansson, *The Adventure of Wrangel Island*, 209.

"February 9 and 25: The woman has been": Stefansson, *The Adventure of Wrangel Island*, 390.

"After six hours": Stefansson, *The Adventure of Wrangel Island*, 218.

"He camped the first night": Stefansson, *The Adventure of Wrangel Island*, 218–219.

"May 27, 1922: I have not said": "Time Drags Heavily and Life Unvaried in Arctic," *Bridgeport Telegram*, November 2, 1923.

"At last!!! Crawford got": Stefansson, *The Adventure of Wrangel Island*, 224.

"I wish to state here": Stefansson, *The Adventure of Wrangel Island*, 391.

"Occasionally I tried likely": Stefansson, *The Adventure of Wrangel Island*, 226–227.

"All along through July": Stefansson, *The Adventure of Wrangel Island*, 227–228.

"Bet with Knight": Milton Galle's diary, August 14, 1922.

"Weather still same": Milton Galle's diary, August 17, 1922.

"Sun out all day": Milton Galle's diary, August 25, 1922 and September 29, 1922.

"We go to bed": Milton Galle's diary, September 12, 1922.

"the suggestion to Crawford": Stefansson, *The Adventure of Wrangel Island*, 320.

MEET LORNE KNIGHT

"Don't a dam [sic] one": Berton, *Prisoners of the North*, 109.

CHAPTER 4: FADING HOPES

"I go for short walk": Stefansson, *The Adventure of Wrangel Island*, 318.

"We had to press": Stefansson, *The Adventure of Wrangel Island*, 354.

"They are just as safe": Stefansson letter to Harry Galle, October 2, 1922.

"C seemed very tired": Milton Galle diary, September 18, 1922.

"The water sky noted": "Failure in Walrus Hunting Is Ominously Significant for Men on Wrangle [sic] Island," *Indianapolis News*, November 24, 1923.

"Everything comes to him": Stefansson, *The Adventure of Wrangel Island*, 237.

"For a long time": "Wrangel Island Party Starts Its Futile Attempt to Reach the Mainland of Siberia," *Indianapolis News*, December 1, 1923.

"On way back K tells": Milton Galle diary, September 28, 1922.

"The woman is doing": Stefansson, *The Adventure of Wrangel Island*, 241.

MEET ALLAN CRAWFORD

"Good jests ought": Leacock, Stephen, "Sermon on Humour," *The Goblin*, February 1921.

"He: Lunch with me?": *The Goblin*, February 1921, 2.

"Always remember the following": Niven, *Ada Blackjack: A True Story of Survival in the Arctic*, 50–51.

CHAPTER 5: TREACHEROUS TREKS

"Crawford and I have": "Wrangel Island Party Starts Its Futile Attempt to Reach the Mainland of Siberia." *The Indianapolis News*, December 1, 1923.

"Lady in the Moon.": Inglis Fletcher Papers, Collection No. 21. East Carolina Manuscript Collection, J. Y. Joyner Library, East Carolina University, Greenville, NC.

"The chief reason for": Diubaldo, *Stefansson and the Canadian Arctic*, 183.

"When I saw how": Diubaldo, *Stefansson and the Canadian Arctic*, 183.

"I will remain here": "Stefansson's Account of Wrangel Tragedy Is an Epic Narrative of Arctic Exploration," *Winnipeg Tribune*, June 13, 1925.

"I don't know what": Pinson, *Alaska's Daughter*.

CHAPTER 6: OH FOR A BEAR!

"The woman is a great": "Losing Struggle Against Disease, Heroism of Eskimo Woman Related in Knight's Diary," *Indianapolis News*, December 14, 1923.

"Ada, Mr. Knight is sick": Stefansson, *The Adventure of Wrangel Island*, 348.

"*I can see that I cannot*": "The Shadow of the End Falls Over Wrangel Island and Adventurers Feel Despair," *Bridgeport Telegram*, November 5, 1923.

"*I feel as though*": "The Shadow of the End," *Bridgeport Telegram*.

"*When I was out*": Stefansson, *The Adventure of Wrangel Island*, 330.

"*The woman says that*": "Losing Struggle Against Disease," *Indianapolis News*.

"*Reading and lying*": Stefansson, *The Adventure of Wrangel Island*, 283.

"*All I want*": Stefansson, *The Adventure of Wrangel Island*, 283.

"*It was a bad time*": Pinson, *Alaska's Daughter*.

"*My dary. I'm going*": "Explorer Dies; Ada Blackjack Is Sole Survivor on Wrangel; Fights Stubbornly for Life," *Bridgeport Telegram*, November 6, 1923.

CHAPTER 7: DOWNWARD SPIRAL

"*as thin as a side*": Stefansson, *The Adventure of Wrangel Island*, 285.

"*I didn't go out*": Ada Blackjack's Diary, April 1, 1923.

"*I said to myself*": Stefansson, *The Adventure of Wrangel Island*, 339.

"*If anything happen*": Ada Blackjack's Diary, April 2, 1923.

"*knight [sic] wants me to go*": Ada Blackjack's Diary, April 2, 1923.

"*And he menitions [sic]*": Ada Blackjack's Diary, April 21, 1923.

"*Caught myself whistling*": "Losing Struggle Against Disease," *Indianapolis News*.

"*He says Black Jack*": Ada Blackjack's Diary, April 21, 1923.

"*Its [sic] hard for women*": Ada Blackjack's Diary, April 21, 1923.

"*I didn't go out today*": Ada Blackjack's Diary, April 24, 1923.

"*This last day of April*": Ada Blackjack's Diary, April 30, 1923.

"*Knight siad [sic] he*": Ada Blackjack's Diary, April 29, 1923.

"*I wish was home*": Ada Blackjack's Diary, May 8, 1923.

"in case I happen to": Ada Blackjack's Diary, June 10, 1923.

"I just write": Ada Blackjack's Diary, June 10, 1923.

"Dear Galle, I didn't": Noice, "The Tragic Crusoes of Wrangel Island," *Literary Digest*, 44, 46.

"He never complained": Pinson, *Alaska's Daughter.*

"What is the matter": Stefansson, *The Adventure of Wrangel Island*, 332.

"Wrangel Island June 23d.": Stefansson, *The Adventure of Wrangel Island*, 289.

"Knight's Poem Here lies": Noice, "The Tragic Crusoes of Wrangel Island," 44.

"I move to the other": Ada Blackjack's Diary, June 22, 1923.

"I found three": Ada Blackjack's Diary, June 26, 1923.

"Hello, somebody!": "Diaries and Records of the Victims of the Wrangel Island Expedition Are Found by Captain Harold Noice and Rescuers," *Indianapolis News*, November 3, 1923.

"This afternoon I hear": Ada Blackjack's Diary, June 28, 1923.

"When I shoot eider": Stefansson, *The Adventure of Wrangel Island*, 343.

"I got a seal": "Explorer Dies; Ada Blackjack Is Sole Survivor," *Bridgeport Telegram*.

"Boam [boom] it went": *Ada Blackjack's Diary*, July 4, 1923.

CHAPTER 8: RESCUE!

"I am glad": Stefansson, *The Adventure of Wrangel Island*, 344.

"All done at one": Ada Blackjack's Diary, July 5, 1923.

"What shall I do": Stefansson, *The Adventure of Wrangel Island*, 343.

"I do not write": Stefansson, *The Adventure of Wrangel Island*, 344.

"I was at the masthead": Harold Noice, "Eskimo Woman's Sole Companion on Wrangel Island for Months Was a Cat," *Indianapolis News*, October 27, 1923.

"It was midnight": Noice, "Eskimo Woman's Sole Companion," *Indianapolis News*.

"I finished my knited [sic]": Ada Blackjack's Diary, August 20, 1923.

"I sprang out": "Crawford Gave Life to Bring Succor to Pal," *Winnipeg Tribune*, September 6, 1923.

"I don't know—much": Harold Noice, "The Tragic Crusoes of Wrangel Island," *Literary Digest*, December 8, 1923, 40.

"I wonder if this": "Noice Lands at Wrangel Only to Hear All Perish," *Winnipeg Tribune*, September 1, 1923.

"Knight—he dead man": Noice, "Eskimo Woman's Sole Companion," *Indianapolis News*.

"After Knight die": Noice, "The Tragic Crusoes of Wrangel Island," *Literary Digest*, 38.

"All he could eat": Noice, "Eskimo Woman's Sole Companion," *Indianapolis News*.

"impossible to realize": Noice, "The Tragic Crusoes of Wrangel Island," *Literary Digest*, 40.

"I have a reindeer": Stefansson, *The Adventure of Wrangel Island*, 342.

"I looked at her": "Diaries and Records of the Victims of the Wrangel Island Expedition," *Indianapolis News*.

"I had hard time": Kenn Harper, "Taissumani: May 29, 1983—The death of Ada Blackjack," www.nunatsiaqonline.ca/archives/60526.

CHAPTER 9: CONFLICT AND CONFUSION

"Sympathy to you all": "Woman Reveals Explorers' Fate," *Ft. Wayne Journal-Gazette*, September 2, 1923.

"This is terrible": "Arctic Island Kills Four Men Who Capture It," *Ottawa Journal*, September 1, 1923.

"Love to you all": "Noice Lands at Wrangel," *Winnipeg Tribune*.

"he [Milton] was full": Stefansson letter to Mrs. Galle, October 11, 1923.

"You are all we have": Niven, *Ada Blackjack*, 301.

"It always makes me": Stefansson, *The Adventure of Wrangel Island*, 346.

"Ada refused to aid": "Ada, Once Heroine of Arctic, Now Painted in Darker Role," *Billings Gazette*, February 22, 1924.

"I still maintain": Harper, "Taissumani: May 29, 1983," www.nunatsiaqonline.ca/archives/60526.

"Knight was sick": "Eskimo Woman Denies Knight Death Charge," *Davenport Democrat and Leader*, March 6, 1924.

"When I got to": Stefansson, *The Adventure of Wrangel Island*, 349.

"I sincerely regret": Stefansson, *The Adventure of Wrangel Island*, 296.

"When I saw how sparse": "Parents of Dead Youth Say Stefansson to Blame," *Ottawa Journal*, April 29, 1925.

"In addition to making": "Parents of Dead Youth," *Ottawa Journal*.

"If you have a gale": Stefansson letter to Mrs. Galle, October 19, 1923.

"During a cloudy": Stefansson letter to Mrs. Galle, October 19, 1923.

"We fail to see": Mrs. Galle's letter to Stefansson, November 6, 1923.

"I think you are right": Stefansson letter to Mrs. Galle, January 12, 1924.

"There are in one": Stefansson letter to Mr. and Mrs. Galle, July 7, 1924.

"I had a hard time": Pinson, *Alaska's Daughter*.

"Ada Blackjack Johnson": Find-a-grave memorial, www.findagrave.com/cgi-bin/Pf.cgi?page_gr&GRid.

"*I consider my mother*": Alexandra J. McClanahan, "The Heroine of Wrangel Island," http://www.litsite.org/index.cfm?section=History-and-Culture&page=Life-in-Alaska&viewpost=2&ContentId=850.

"*a small token*": Harper, "Taissumani: May 29, 1983," www.nunatsiaqonline.cal/archives/6526.

SOURCES

BOOKS

Berton, Pierre. *Prisoners of the North.* New York: Carroll & Graf Publishers, 2004.

Cummins, Joseph. *Cast Away.* Australia: Murdoch Books, 2008.

Diubaldo, Richard J. *Stefansson and the Canadian Arctic.* Montreal: MGill-Queen's University Press, 1998.

Jocelyn, Marthe. *Scribbling Women: True Tales from Astonishing Lives.* Canada: Tundra Books, 2011.

Montgomery, Richard G. *Pechuck: Lorne Knight's Adventures in the Arctic.* New York: Dodd, Mead and Company, 1932.

Niven, Jennifer. *Ada Blackjack: A True Story of Survival in the Arctic.* New York: Hyperion, 2003.

Noice, Harold. *With Stefansson in the Arctic.* New York: Dodd, Mad, & Company, Publishers, 1925.

Pinson, Elizabeth Bernhardt. *Alaska's Daughter: An Eskimo Memoir of the Early Twentieth Century*. Logan, UT: Utah State University Press, 1912. http://digitalcommons.usu.edu/usupress_pubs/84.

Stefansson, Vilhjalmur. *The Adventure of Wrangel Island*. New York: The Macmillan Company, 1925.

Stefansson, Vilhjalmur. *The Friendly Arctic: The Story of Five Years in Polar Regions*. New York: The Macmillan Company, 1921.

LETTERS AND TELEGRAMS

Alma Galle to Vilhjalmur Stefansson, November 6, 1923.

Milton Galle to mother, no date on telegram.

Milton Galle to parents, August 15, 1921

Milton Galle to Stefansson, September 8, 1921.

Vilhjalmur Stefansson to Harry Galle, October 2, 1922.

Vilhjalmur Stefansson to Alma Galle, October 19, 1923.

Vilhjalmur Stefansson to Alma Galle, January 12, 1924

Vilhjalmur Stefansson to Alma Galle, July 7, 1924.

Vilhjalmur Stefansson to Alma Galle, November 13, 1924.

Vilhjalmur Stefansson to Harry and Alma Galle, October 11, 1923.

All materials were provided to the author from the private research collection of Lynn Thompson.

DIARIES

Ada Blackjack's Diary. The Stefansson Collection. Rauner Special Collections Library, Dartmouth College Library.

Milton Galle's Diary. The Stefansson Collection. Rauner Special Collections Library, Dartmouth College Library.

INDEX

Abrahams, Joe, 152

Adventure of Wrangel Island, The
  (Stefansson), 169

Alahuk, Alik (Alex), 21

Allen, Alexander, 134

Anderson, 23–24

Arctic fox, 110*ph*, 111

Arctic hysteria, 34

Baird, Evelyn Schwartz, 26

Bartlett, Captain R. A. "Bob,"
  17, 22

Belvedere, 23

Bernard, Captain Joe, 77, 78–79

Blackjack, Ada
  after Knight's death, 125–128
  arrival of on island, 16,
    29–30
  beginning of expedition and,
    11–12
  birth of, 1
  birthday of, 57, 119
  childhood of, 1–2
  Crawford and, 31–32
  death of, 171
  decision to join expedition
    and, 8, 10
  diary of, 113, 117–119, 120–
    121
  disappearance of, 36–37
  formal recognition of,
    171–172

health of, 115–116

with Knight, 105–110, 112–114, 117

Knight's family and, 155–156, 158

later life of, 169–171

learning to shoot, 120

letter to Galle from, 121–122

marriage of, 2

Noice and, 162–164

photographs of, 129*ph*, 145*ph*, 150*ph*, 159*ph*

polar bears and, 1, 8, 44, 50, 131–132

portrait of, 6*ph*

relationship with men and, 37–38

rescue of, 137–141, 143–144, 147, 149

in Seattle, 155

Stefansson's book and, 169

strange behavior of, 33–35, 50

trapping and, 108

Blackjack, Bennett (son), 2–3, 11, 116, 121, 144, 149, 158, 160, 169–170

Blackjack, Jack, 2, 151

camera, invention of, 157

Canadian Arctic Expedition, 22

cats, 13

see also Nicki (cat); Vic (cat)

Chautauqua lecture circuit. *see* Circuit Chautauqua

Christmas, 50–51, 84

Circuit Chautauqua, 24, 25, 26, 45, 68, 88, 102

clothing, 10, 12–13

Copper Inuits, 20–21

Crawford, Allan Rudyard

Ada and, 31–32

attempted journey to Siberia and, 91–96, 98

background of, 87–88, 90

claiming of island and, 17, 28

departure of, 99–100

family of, 165

news of death of, 151

photograph of, 55*ph*, 92*ph*

purchase of shares by, 7

selection of, 4–5

Crawford, J. T., 151

Dartmouth College, 26

Davydov, Captain B. D., 146

Delutuk, Ada. *see* Blackjack, Ada

Delutuk, Fina (sister), 1, 149

Delutuk, Rita (sister). *see* McCaffery, Rita (sister)

Discovery (Stefansson), 26

dogs, 40–41, 51, 52*ph*

see also Strongheart

Donaldson, 132–133, 133*ph*, 134, 135–136, 147, 149

dory, 72*ph*, 73–74

Doubtful Harbour, 28, 59*ph*, 82, 137

Eastman, George, 157

fireman, ship's, 102

Fletcher, Mrs. Inglis, 158, 160, 169

flowers, 58

food
    description of, 62, 63
    search for, 39–40
    shortage of, 64–65, 71–72, 75, 91, 92, 98
    storage of, 82
    see also polar bears; seals; walruses

fox, Arctic, 110ph, 111

Friendly Arctic, The (Stefansson), 26

frostbite, 95

Gallé, Émile, 45, 47

Galle, Milton Robert Harvey
    Ada and, 37–38
    Ada's letter to, 121–122
    attempted journey to Siberia and, 98, 99–100
    background of, 45–46, 48
    cooking by, 61–62
    diary of, 62–64
    family of, 154–155
    lack of salary for, 4–5, 7–8
    news of death of, 152
    photograph of, 85ph
    selection of, 4–5
    Stefansson and, 24

Stefansson's letters to family of, 165–169

glassmaking, 47

Goblin, The, 88, 89

Gregory IX, Pope, 13

Hammer, Captain Jack, 11, 14, 18

Herschel Island, 20, 23, 68–69

house, 35–36

hysteria, Arctic, 34

ilhook (retriever), 52–53

Inuit language, 103

Johnson, Billy (son), 169, 170, 171–172

Johnson, George, 169, 170

Jones, Delphine, 103–104

Jordan, E. R., 3, 149

Karluk, 22, 23, 59, 101

Klengenberg, Captain "Charlie," 20, 21

Knight, Errol Lorne
    Ada and, 29, 38
    Ada's fear of, 32, 37
    after others' departure, 105–110, 112–114
    attempted journey to Siberia and, 91–96
    background of, 66–69
    burial of, 142ph, 143
    death of, 123–124, 125, 141

description of island by,
    28–29
diary of, 18, 152, 153, 167
exploration by, 59–60
family of, 158, 162–163
on food situation, 99
health of, 60–61, 84, 106,
    112–113, 114, 115, 117,
    119–120, 122–123
Maurer and, 103
news of death of, 152
Noice and, 137
photograph of, 94*ph*
poem by, 124–125
purchase of shares by, 7
selection of, 4–5
Stefansson and, 24
Knight, Joe, 66–67
Knight, John, 152, 155–156
Kodak, 157

Lady in the Moon, The, 96, 97
Lane, Captain Louis L., 24,
    67–68
lantern slides, 70
Leacock, Stephen, 89
Leffingwell-Mikkelsen
    expedition, 20
lemmings, 16*ph*, 111

magic lantern, 70
Maurer, Frederick W.
    attempted journey to Siberia
        and, 98

background of, 101–104
departure of, 99–100
photograph of, 96*ph*
purchase of shares by, 7
selection of, 4–5
Stefansson and, 24
Stefansson's letter to family
    of, 151
McCaffery, Rita (sister), 1, 121,
    149
Melville, Herman, 68
Moby-Dick (Melville), 68
Montgomery, Richard, 68

Nanook, 43
    see also polar bears
Nicki (cat), 101
Noice, Harold
    accusations made by, 162–
        164
    Ada's rescue by, 138–140, 147
    en route to Wrangel Island,
        132–133, 134
    Knight and, 141–143
    Knight's diary and, 152, 153
    Knight's family and, 152
    search for expedition party
        by, 135, 136–137
    Stefansson and, 151, 154

Pan-American Airways, 26
Pannigabluk, Fanny, 21
*Pechuck: The Arctic Adventures of
    Lorne Knight*, 68

Polar Bear, 67–69, 137
polar bears
  Ada's fear of, 1, 8, 44, 50
  close encounter with, 41–44
  Eskimo beliefs about, 43, 49
  first encounter with, 31
  hunting of, 33, 40, 53–55, 82
  legend of, 49–50
  photograph of, 30*ph*
provisions, 12–14

Red October, 146
relief ship
  expectation of, 57, 75, 80
  ice conditions and, 77–79
  lack of funding for, 75–77
  see also Donaldson
retriever, 52–53
Rodgers Harbour, 15, 37, 60, 136

scurvy, 23, 69, 80, 81, 84, 95–96, 106, 107, 109, 115, 123
Sea Wolf, 78
seal pokes, 61
seals, hunting of, 52–53, 55–56, 57, 61
shamans, 8, 9
ship's fireman, 102
Silver Wave, 10–11, 14, 27, 151
Skeleton River, 59–60
snow blindness, 115–116
snow blocks, 35*ph*
Sperber, Gisela, 170

Stefansson, Vilhjalmur
  Ada and, 158
  background of, 19–20
  Canadian Arctic Expedition and, 21, 22, 23–24
  Circuit Chautauqua and, 24, 26
  claiming of island and, 17, 27
  Copper Inuits and, 20–21
  Crawford and, 87–88, 90
  Donaldson and, 134
  failure of expedition and, 151, 153–154, 164–165
  Galle and, 45–46, 48
  Galle's family and, 165–169
  Karluk and, 24
  Knight and, 67–69
  Knight's and Crawford's letters to, 92–93
  Knight's diary and, 153
  lack of concern of, 79–80
  Maurer and, 103, 104
  Noice and, 137, 164
  organization of expedition by, 3–5
  purpose of expedition and, 6–7, 8
  relief ship and, 75–77
Storkerson, 23–24
Strongheart, 160, 161
supplies, 12–14

Taylor, Alfred J. T., 88, 153
Teddy Bear, 24, 48, 77–79, 78*ph*

tents, 29
trapping camp, 37, 41–42, 60
traps, Ada's learning about, 108
tuberculosis, 2, 3
tundra, 58, 59*ph*

umiak, 14–15

Vic (cat), 11–12, 54, 126, 129*ph*,
    141
Victoria, 5, 11–12
vitamin C, 123

walruses, 39–40, 39*ph*, 71–75
Wells, Charles, 144, 146, 174

whaling, 68
Wrangel expedition
    arrival of on island, 15–16
    departure of, 11–12
    fundraising for, 3–4, 24
    members of, 4–5
    purpose of, 5–7, 8
Wrangel Island
    description of, 15, 28
    as nature sanctuary, 173–174
    proclamation claiming,
        16–18, 27
    replacement team on, 144
    Russian claim on, 146–147
Wright, Orville, 76, 134